Moon Method Diary 2024

Created by Anna Maria Whitehead

© COPYRIGHT ANNA MARIA WHITEHEAD 2024

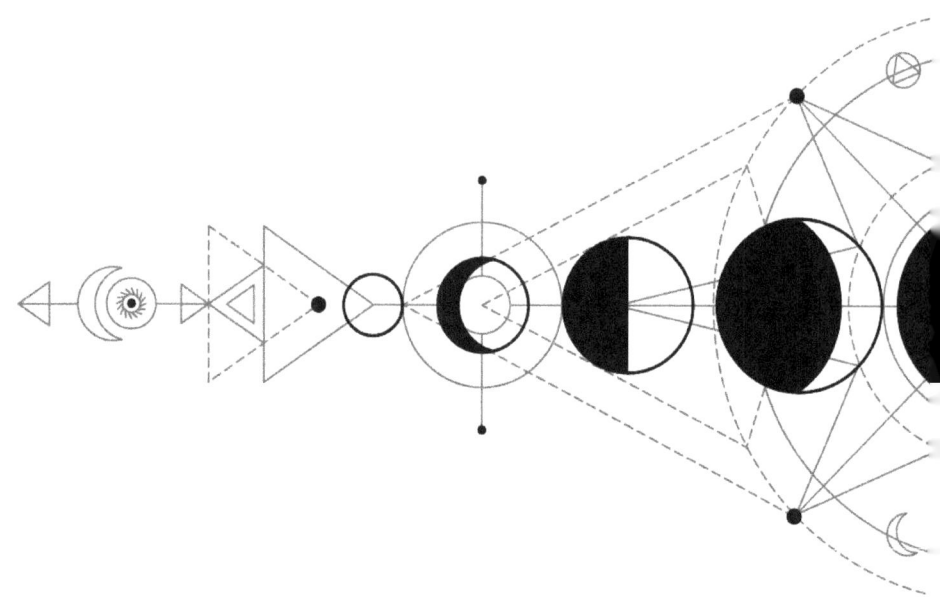

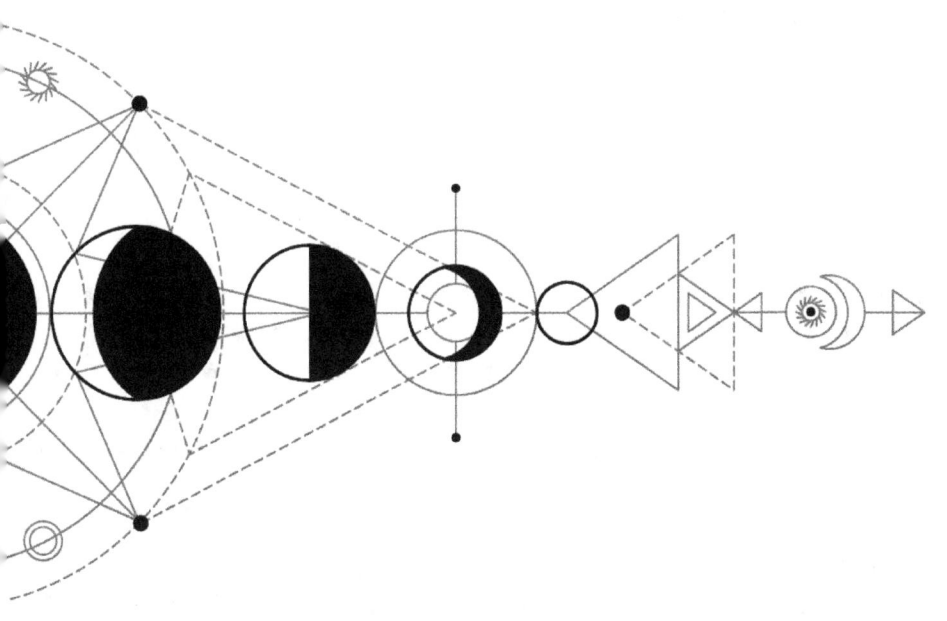

The process of self-discovery deepens and strengthens your spiritual connection to life, Earth and the universe. Gradually, you will come to your own truths, and gradually you will let them go, as you embrace deeper, more profound realisations. Every precious, miraculous moment of your life has the capacity to transform you

Leela – Sacred Earth Journal

Phases of the moon

New Moon
New beginnings and intention setting

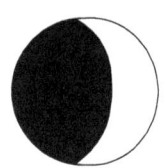

Waxing Moon
Put plans into action

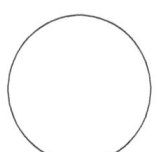

Full Moon
Gratitude for all you have received

Waning Moon
Release anything that no longer serves you

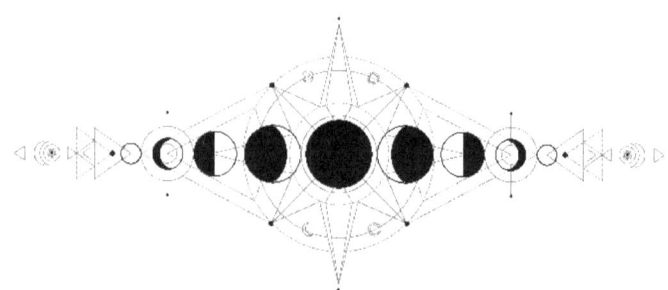

Working with the moon

Live in sync with nature to manifest your best life.

Do you ever feel overwhelmed with to-do lists? Do you experience days when you have planned to see a friend, only to find when the day comes along you do not feel like socialising?

The secret is being able to forward plan our schedules by having an idea of where our energy levels will be at different times throughout the month. Nature can help you to be your most productive self, when you listen. Use the varying energy of the moon's cycles to your benefit. The demands of our modern world often make us feel that we need to be on top of our game every day. Being busy is almost treated as a badge of honour, but we are not supposed to be operating at one hundred percent every day of the month. We are cyclical beings. Rest and alone time also need to be honoured and included on our schedules with the same importance as any business meeting.

When we rest, we recharge and become our most productive selves. During the New Moon we set intentions for the month ahead, we are then free to move forward focussing on our goals, with a renewed clarity on what we want and heightened energy to get us there.

The aim of this diary is to help you organise busy schedules whilst avoiding burnout and feeling overwhelmed. When life flows easily, creativity and happiness will come to you in abundance.

Wishing you a very happy, productive year full of joy.

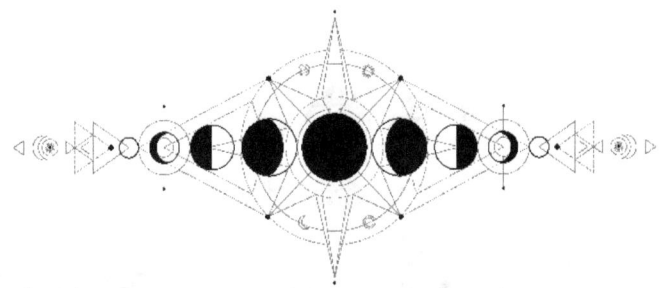

A New Moon is a monthly rebirth, a time for new beginnings, ideas and creativity. An opportunity to set your intentions. This is a perfect time to spend alone journaling your thoughts and practicing self care which will mean different things to all of you. Perhaps a morning meditation or an evening bubble bath is all it takes, but whatever it is, make sure to take some time for yourself. In the silence you will receive the intuitive guidance you need. Take some time to set your intentions for the month ahead.

Clear Quartz, a cleansing crystal perfect for clearing the mind and aiding in meditation.

The Waxing Moon asks you to act upon the ideas you received during the new moon. This is a perfect time for socialising and communication, so scheduling in meetings would be good during a waxing moon, but be careful not to burnout, eat well during this moon and avoid anything not so good for you.

Citrine, a wonderful crystal for manifesting abundance.

A Full Moon is a good time to check in with the intentions you set under the new moon. Consider what finishing touches you need to look at to get you to your goals. Work with your intuition and gut feelings. Energies are very high under this powerful moon phase, so you will have energy for meeting with friends, but you may prefer to use this energy to be at home burning your favourite incense whilst meditating and tuning into your highest self. Full moons are a great time to cleanse the body and mind.

Moonstone, helps to connect to your inner goddess and true meaning.

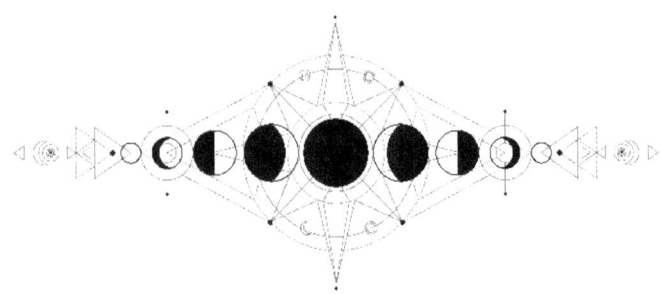

The Waning Moon calls you to release that which does not serve you. Pay attention to anything that has stood in the way of your goals and dreams. This is a perfect time to organise, throw things away, consider if you have any toxic elements in your life. Do you need to get rid of any particular bad habits? Now would be the time to start looking at that. Let go of unwanted energy and release.

Rhodonite, a healer related to the heart chakra which helps with forgiveness and releases self-destructive tendencies to help with healing at a soul level.

How amazing is the moon!? She provides us with the chance to start afresh every month and use her energy to guide us. These points refer to how the moon affects us collectively, but each moon will affect us all slightly differently depending on our own birth charts. You may wish to dive deeper into this with an astrologer as it can be helpful for introspection and making sense of our experiences as we move throughout the year.

A little side note about working with and charting menstrual cycles along side the moon cycles. Start on day one of your cycle and write a note on each day about anything you feel you would like to chart, particularly your emotions and energy levels.

It is good practice to chart our cycles, and this includes those of us who don't have a menstrual cycle. It can still be very beneficial to chart our states of being on a daily basis allowing us to notice any patterns over the period of a few months. This is a useful tool in getting to know subtleties about yourself. You can then use this information to work in harmony with your inner ebbs and flows. For example if you see that you are always exhausted on day twenty, but full of life on day twelve then you can use this information to your advantage.

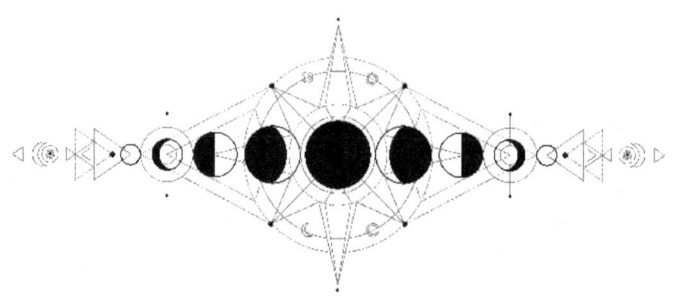

Honouring the seasons
Paying close attention to the seasons and creating rituals around them helps us in turn to honour ourselves. We are nature. We are cyclical beings. When we move with the natural rhythms of our Earth, we learn to live in a flow state, in the present. As each season moves into the next on the wheel of the year, we can celebrate these changes outside and inside of ourselves. Equinoxes and solstices allow us to feel at one with the seasons and remind us to check in with ourselves, so rather than mindlessly racing through the year wondering how another one flew by so quickly, working with the seasons can add focus and clarity to these 366 days (don't forget it's a leap year!).

Spring Equinox 20th March
A time when light and dark come into balance and nature blooms with life. Use this time to think about what seeds you want to sow in your own life. How do you want to use this new vital energy to manifest abundance? Spring shows us how to be patient whilst we wait for the little buds to blossom. Emulate nature in this way and be easy on yourself if you are waiting for your manifestations to come to fruition. Try and spend at least ten minutes every day with your bare feet touching the Earth. Take as much time in nature as you can, pausing to pay attention to spring as she emerges from the dark winter. Close your eyes and take in the sounds of nature all around you. Spend time journaling on your goals for the remainder of the year. Are there steps you can now take as you leave winter behind you to get ready to step into the light of spring?

Ritual ideas: Cleanse your space with frankincense or incense of your choice, do a grounding meditation such as a root chakra meditation by imagining that your feet root firmly into the Earth, you could sit with your back against a tree for twenty minutes connecting with the Earth's energy, followed by a cleansing bath with Epsom salts and rose petals.

Summer Solstice 20th June
In the northern hemisphere the Earth's axis is tilted at its closest point from the sun. This is the longest day, and shortest night. Nature is in full bloom all around us and inspires us to put our creative ideas into practice and bring projects to life. Use the heightened energy of the solstice to create and be inspired.

Ritual Ideas: Get outside, walk barefoot through a forest, hold a fire circle with friends. Celebrate nature and each other. Eat fresh food from the Earth and give thanks for all that she provides us. Write lists of everything you are grateful for. What is showing up in abundance for you? Stop and pause to give thanks for it. Get up at sunrise to honour the sun. Perhaps incorporate a yoga session or whatever suits you to move your body. Get creative with your celebrations and make them your own.

Autumn Equinox 22nd September
The first day of autumn is a time for releasing. Get clear on what no longer serves you, and just like the trees who shed their leaves, allow yourself to let go. The days will begin to get shorter and nature invites you to retreat inwards to rejuvenate. There is a different level of energy that we are now heading into, and one of the best ways to honour that time is to reflect on the year so far, and ask what you need to shed to move forward.

Ritual ideas: Write a list of anything you don't want to take with you as we move into this next part of the year, make a bonfire and burn the list. Take a long walk and notice the changes in nature all around you and take home some moss and wood to make an altar for the Earth goddess Gaia. As the nights get shorter and the air gets colder embrace the change in energy and the subtle whispers calling you inwards.

Winter Solstice 21st December
Celebrate the cyclical nature of our world on the longest night before the sun is renewed once more. The winter solstice welcomes a slower pace, honour that. Reclaim the stillness. The darkness of winter can be difficult, try and notice the beauty of the sparse trees and frosty mornings. Treat yourself to comforting foods and special time with loved ones playing board games and embrace the slower, quieter, darker days.

Ritual ideas: Spend some time in silence reflecting on the year so far and your dreams for the year ahead. Head to a beauty spot that you have a connection with and reflect on any changes to this area during winter. Wrap up warm and enjoy a fire, the flames can be very meditative and healing. Shamans say that fire allows for rapid transformation. Make the most of the darkness and any revelations it has helped bring to light.

Wheel of the year

* Yule - December 21st
Yule is the winter festival celebrating the winter solstice and the returning of the light.

* Imbolc - February 1st
This festival marks the beginning of spring. Goddess Bridgid is celebrated during with feasts and fires. Green candles are lit in her honour.

* Ostara - March 20th
A solar holiday where we welcome the returning warmth of spring. Goddess Eostre is honoured with alters of flowers, eggs and seeds.

* Beltane - May 1st
The half way mark between the spring equinox and summer solstice. We give thanks to the fertility of the land.

* Litha - June 20th
The longest day of the year. Vikings would pray to Freyja for an abundant harvest and ceremonial plants are used around midsummer bonfires.

* Lammas - August 1st
Represents the midway point between summer and autumn. The time of the first harvest.

* Mabon - September 22nd
The second harvest which lands on the autumn equinox.

* Samhian - October 31st
Better known as halloween this is the Celtic new year and the final harvest.

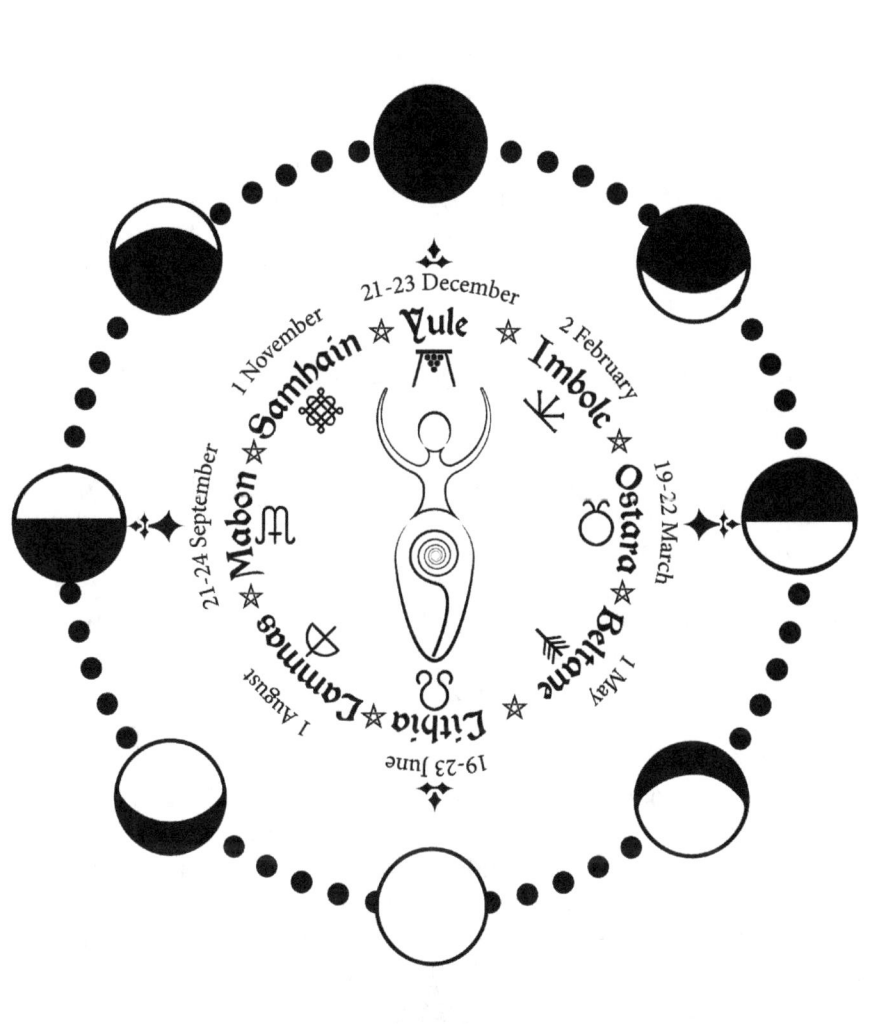

Three Ways to manifest your dreams

New Years resolutions are a cultural norm for many of us, but often we find it difficult to commit. It may be that the depth of winter just isn't the right time for making big decisions for the next twelve months. Some of us prefer to write down our visions for the year around the spring equinox when the world around us is coming to life.

There is no right or wrong. Fill in the goals pages at whatever time of year feels right to you.

There are many ways to bring our creative visions to life, and you will find more than one way to manifest your dreams in this diary. Yearly goal setting, seasonal visions plus a vision board.

On the opposite page you can write out your main yearly goal, with space to break it down. Work out what you need to do daily, weekly and monthly to get you to where you want to be by 2025.

There is also space for seasonal inspiration. Spend some time each equinox and solstice quietly observing and making space for inspiration to come through. Take some time out with a warm drink, a candle and something that represents the season, perhaps a flower, certain colours or a crystal, and allow yourself to visualise your desires for the season ahead. As mother Earth moves through her cycles we often find that ideas come to us that we never would have thought of during the darker days around New Year. Manifesting alongside the seasons adds a beautiful dimension to making our dreams a reality.

My main yearly goal is: _____

To achieve this goal by 2025, I will create the following habits to get myself there.

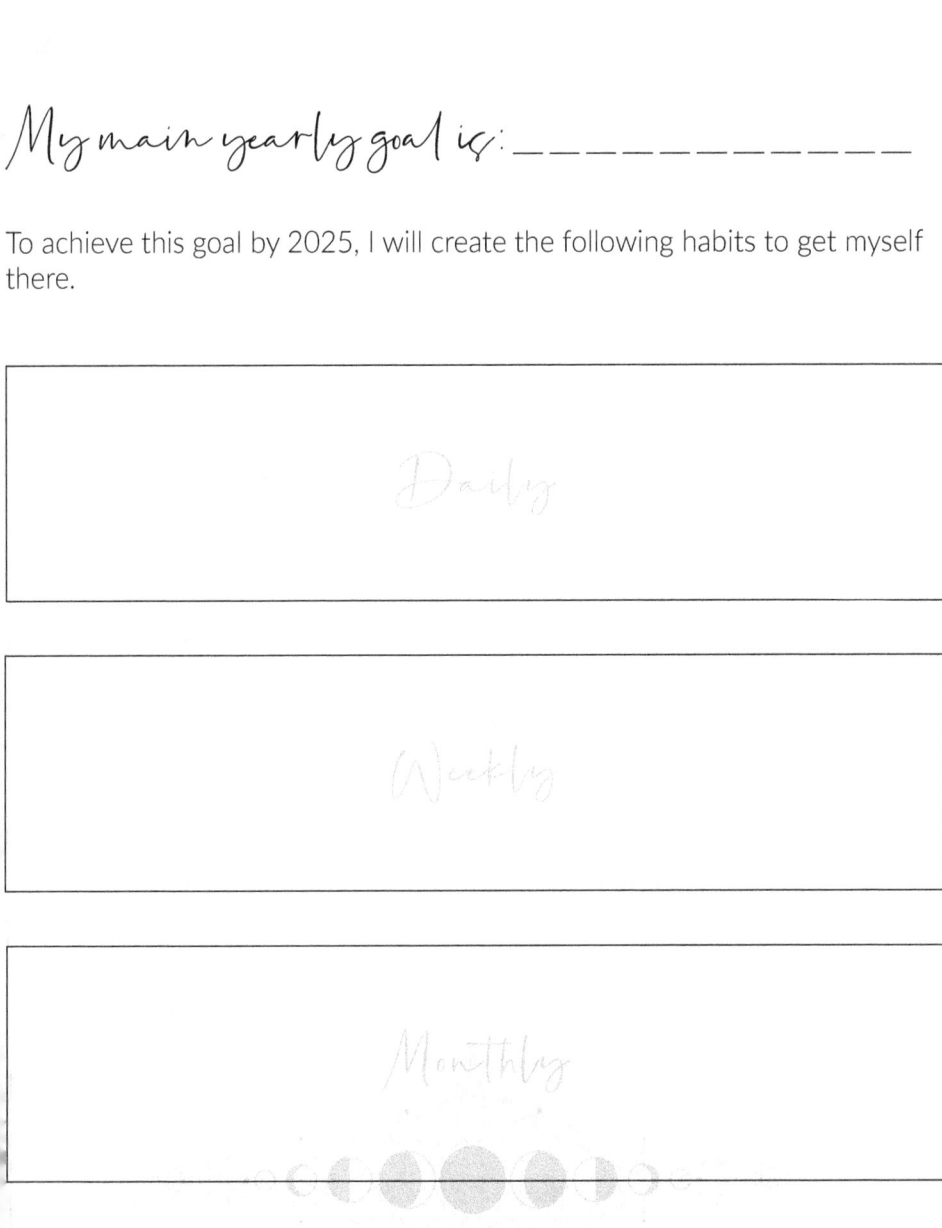

Seasonal Vision for 2024

Use this space to write any ideas that come to you throughout the year. From Inspirational business ideas, passion projects or perhaps countries you want to visit.

Winter

Spring

Summer

Autumn

Vision board

Use this space to paint, doodle or cut pictures out of magazines. Whatever works for you. The goal is to create a powerful visualisation tool to aid in manifesting your dreams. You can look at this every day to bring your 2024 goals to life.

Share your vision with us on Instagram @the_moonmethod

"Practice listening to your intuition, your inner voice; ask questions; be curious; see what you see; hear what you hear; and then act upon what you know to be true. These intuitive powers were given to your soul at birth."

— Clarissa Pinkola Estés

Listen to your intuition

Make notes here when you notice that you have listened to or ignored your inner compass. The more we pay attention the more attuned we become...

January 2024

Notes	Monday	Tuesday	Wednesday
	1	2	3
	8	9	10
	15	16	17
	22	23	24
	29	30	31

Thursday	Friday	Saturday	Sunday
4	5	6	7
11 ●	12	13	14
18 ◐	19	20	21
25 ○	26	27	28
1	2	3	4

January
Athena

ATHENA

Goddess of wisdom and guardian of Greece

She gifted the city of Athens with an olive tree which provided wood, oil and food as a symbol of peace.

Though she is well known today as the goddess of war, she was wise, generous and loyal. She did have the ability to be a fierce warrior goddess when necessary. She knew when to stand in her power and also when to cultivate calm and peace.

People call on her energy today for for protection, healing, strength and courage.

Book: Warrior Goddess Training: Become the Woman You Are Meant To Be by Heatherash Amara
Song: Blessings by Lila
Moon Phase: New Moon
Crystal: Lapis Lazuli

My Vision for January

Monday | 1 January 2024 - Waning Gibbous

6:00	Today's quick wins	
7:00		
8:00		
9:00		
10:00		
11:00	Health and nutrition	
12:00		
13:00		
14:00	Today, I am grateful for...	
15:00		
16:00		
17:00	Today's self care	
18:00		
19:00		
20:00	Chart your cycle	
21:00		
22:00		
23:00	Positive affirmation	

Notes

Tuesday | 2 January 2024 - Waning Gibbous

6:00	**Today's quick wins**
7:00	
8:00	
9:00	
10:00	
11:00	**Health and nutrition**
12:00	
13:00	
14:00	**Today, I am grateful for...**
15:00	
16:00	
17:00	**Today's self care**
18:00	
19:00	
20:00	**Chart your cycle**
21:00	
22:00	
23:00	**Positive affirmation**

Notes

Wednesday | 3 January 2024 - Last Quarter

6:00		Today's quick wins	
7:00			
8:00			
9:00			
10:00			
11:00		Health and nutrition	
12:00			
13:00			
14:00		Today, I am grateful for...	
15:00			
16:00			
17:00		Today's self care	
18:00			
19:00			
20:00		Chart your cycle	
21:00			
22:00			
23:00		Positive affirmation	

Notes

Thursday | 4 January 2024 - Last Quarter

6:00	**Today's quick wins**
7:00	
8:00	
9:00	
10:00	
11:00	**Health and nutrition**
12:00	
13:00	
14:00	**Today, I am grateful for...**
15:00	
16:00	
17:00	**Today's self care**
18:00	
19:00	
20:00	**Chart your cycle**
21:00	
22:00	
23:00	**Positive affirmation**
Notes	

Friday | 5 January 2024 - Waning Crescent

6:00		Today's quick wins
7:00		
8:00		
9:00		
10:00		
11:00		Health and nutrition
12:00		
13:00		
14:00		Today, I am grateful for...
15:00		
16:00		
17:00		Today's self care
18:00		
19:00		
20:00		Chart your cycle
21:00		
22:00		
23:00		Positive affirmation
Notes		

Saturday | 6 January 2024 - Waning Crescent

6:00	**Today's quick wins**
7:00	
8:00	
9:00	
10:00	
11:00	**Health and nutrition**
12:00	
13:00	
14:00	**Today, I am grateful for...**
15:00	
16:00	
17:00	**Today's self care**
18:00	
19:00	
20:00	**Chart your cycle**
21:00	
22:00	
23:00	**Positive affirmation**

Notes

Sunday | 7 January 2024 - Waning Crescent

6:00	**Today's quick wins**
7:00	
8:00	
9:00	
10:00	
11:00	**Health and nutrition**
12:00	
13:00	
14:00	**Today, I am grateful for...**
15:00	
16:00	
17:00	**Today's self care**
18:00	
19:00	
20:00	**Chart your cycle**
21:00	
22:00	
23:00	**Positive affirmation**

Notes

Monday | 8 January 2024 - Waning Crescent

6:00	Today's quick wins
7:00	
8:00	
9:00	
10:00	
11:00	Health and nutrition
12:00	
13:00	
14:00	Today, I am grateful for...
15:00	
16:00	
17:00	Today's self care
18:00	
19:00	
20:00	Chart your cycle
21:00	
22:00	
23:00	Positive affirmation

Notes

Tuesday | 9 January 2024 - Waning Crescent

6:00		**Today's quick wins**	
7:00			
8:00			
9:00			
10:00			
11:00		**Health and nutrition**	
12:00			
13:00			
14:00		**Today, I am grateful for...**	
15:00			
16:00			
17:00		**Today's self care**	
18:00			
19:00			
20:00		**Chart your cycle**	
21:00			
22:00			
23:00		**Positive affirmation**	

Notes

Wednesday | 10 January 2024 - Waning Crescent

6:00		Today's quick wins	
7:00			
8:00			
9:00			
10:00			
11:00		Health and nutrition	
12:00			
13:00			
14:00		Today, I am grateful for...	
15:00			
16:00			
17:00		Today's self care	
18:00			
19:00			
20:00		Chart your cycle	
21:00			
22:00			
23:00		Positive affirmation	
Notes			

Thursday | 11 January 2024 - New Moon in Capricorn 11.57 GMT

6:00		**Today's quick wins**
7:00		
8:00		
9:00		
10:00		
11:00		**Health and nutrition**
12:00		
13:00		
14:00		**Today, I am grateful for…**
15:00		
16:00		
17:00		**Today's self care**
18:00		
19:00		
20:00		**Chart your cycle**
21:00		
22:00		
23:00		**Positive affirmation**

Notes

Friday | 12 January 2024 - Waxing Crescent

6:00	**Today's quick wins**
7:00	
8:00	
9:00	
10:00	
11:00	**Health and nutrition**
12:00	
13:00	
14:00	**Today, I am grateful for...**
15:00	
16:00	
17:00	**Today's self care**
18:00	
19:00	
20:00	**Chart your cycle**
21:00	
22:00	
23:00	**Positive affirmation**

Notes

Saturday | 13 January 2024 - Waxing Crescent

6:00	**Today's quick wins**
7:00	
8:00	
9:00	
10:00	
11:00	**Health and nutrition**
12:00	
13:00	
14:00	**Today, I am grateful for...**
15:00	
16:00	
17:00	**Today's self care**
18:00	
19:00	
20:00	**Chart your cycle**
21:00	
22:00	
23:00	**Positive affirmation**

Notes

Sunday | 14 January 2024 - Waxing Crescent

6:00	**Today's quick wins**
7:00	
8:00	
9:00	
10:00	
11:00	**Health and nutrition**
12:00	
13:00	
14:00	**Today, I am grateful for...**
15:00	
16:00	
17:00	**Today's self care**
18:00	
19:00	
20:00	**Chart your cycle**
21:00	
22:00	
23:00	**Positive affirmation**

Notes

Monday | 15 January 2024 - Waxing Crescent

6:00		Today's quick wins
7:00		
8:00		
9:00		
10:00		
11:00		Health and nutrition
12:00		
13:00		
14:00		Today, I am grateful for...
15:00		
16:00		
17:00		Today's self care
18:00		
19:00		
20:00		Chart your cycle
21:00		
22:00		
23:00		Positive affirmation
Notes		

Tuesday | 16 January 2024 - Waxing Crescent

6:00		**Today's quick wins**	
7:00			
8:00			
9:00			
10:00			
11:00		**Health and nutrition**	
12:00			
13:00			
14:00		**Today, I am grateful for...**	
15:00			
16:00			
17:00		**Today's self care**	
18:00			
19:00			
20:00		**Chart your cycle**	
21:00			
22:00			
23:00		**Positive affirmation**	

Notes

Wednesday | 17 January 2024 - Waxing Crescent

6:00		**Today's quick wins**	
7:00			
8:00			
9:00			
10:00			
11:00		**Health and nutrition**	
12:00			
13:00			
14:00		**Today, I am grateful for...**	
15:00			
16:00			
17:00		**Today's self care**	
18:00			
19:00			
20:00		**Chart your cycle**	
21:00			
22:00			
23:00		**Positive affirmation**	
Notes			

Thursday | 18 January 2024 - First Quarter

6:00	Today's quick wins
7:00	
8:00	
9:00	
10:00	
11:00	Health and nutrition
12:00	
13:00	
14:00	Today, I am grateful for...
15:00	
16:00	
17:00	Today's self care
18:00	
19:00	
20:00	Chart your cycle
21:00	
22:00	
23:00	Positive affirmation

Notes

Friday | 19 January 2024 - Waxing Gibbous

6:00	**Today's quick wins**
7:00	
8:00	
9:00	
10:00	
11:00	**Health and nutrition**
12:00	
13:00	
14:00	**Today, I am grateful for...**
15:00	
16:00	
17:00	**Today's self care**
18:00	
19:00	
20:00	**Chart your cycle**
21:00	
22:00	
23:00	**Positive affirmation**

Notes

Saturday | 20 January 2024 - Waxing Gibbous

6:00	**Today's quick wins**
7:00	
8:00	
9:00	
10:00	
11:00	**Health and nutrition**
12:00	
13:00	
14:00	**Today, I am grateful for...**
15:00	
16:00	
17:00	**Today's self care**
18:00	
19:00	
20:00	**Chart your cycle**
21:00	
22:00	
23:00	**Positive affirmation**

Notes

Sunday | 21 January 2024 - Waxing Gibbous

6:00		**Today's quick wins**	
7:00			
8:00			
9:00			
10:00			
11:00		**Health and nutrition**	
12:00			
13:00			
14:00		**Today, I am grateful for...**	
15:00			
16:00			
17:00		**Today's self care**	
18:00			
19:00			
20:00		**Chart your cycle**	
21:00			
22:00			
23:00		**Positive affirmation**	
Notes			

Monday | 22 January 2024 - Waxing Gibbous

6:00	**Today's quick wins**
7:00	
8:00	
9:00	
10:00	
11:00	**Health and nutrition**
12:00	
13:00	
14:00	**Today, I am grateful for...**
15:00	
16:00	
17:00	**Today's self care**
18:00	
19:00	
20:00	**Chart your cycle**
21:00	
22:00	
23:00	**Positive affirmation**

Notes

Tuesday | 23 January 2024 - Waxing Gibbous

6:00	**Today's quick wins**
7:00	
8:00	
9:00	
10:00	
11:00	**Health and nutrition**
12:00	
13:00	
14:00	**Today, I am grateful for...**
15:00	
16:00	
17:00	**Today's self care**
18:00	
19:00	
20:00	**Chart your cycle**
21:00	
22:00	
23:00	**Positive affirmation**
Notes	

Wednesday | 24 January 2024 - Waxing Gibbous

6:00	**Today's quick wins**
7:00	
8:00	
9:00	
10:00	
11:00	**Health and nutrition**
12:00	
13:00	
14:00	**Today, I am grateful for...**
15:00	
16:00	
17:00	**Today's self care**
18:00	
19:00	
20:00	**Chart your cycle**
21:00	
22:00	
23:00	**Positive affirmation**

Notes

Thursday | 25 January 2024 - Full Moon in Leo 17.53 GMT

6:00		**Today's quick wins**
7:00		
8:00		
9:00		
10:00		
11:00		**Health and nutrition**
12:00		
13:00		
14:00		**Today, I am grateful for...**
15:00		
16:00		
17:00		**Today's self care**
18:00		
19:00		
20:00		**Chart your cycle**
21:00		
22:00		
23:00		**Positive affirmation**

Notes

Friday | 26 January 2024 - Waning Gibbous

6:00	**Today's quick wins**
7:00	
8:00	
9:00	
10:00	
11:00	**Health and nutrition**
12:00	
13:00	
14:00	**Today, I am grateful for...**
15:00	
16:00	
17:00	**Today's self care**
18:00	
19:00	
20:00	**Chart your cycle**
21:00	
22:00	
23:00	**Positive affirmation**

Notes

Saturday | 27 January 2024 - Waning Gibbous

6:00	**Today's quick wins**
7:00	
8:00	
9:00	
10:00	
11:00	**Health and nutrition**
12:00	
13:00	
14:00	**Today, I am grateful for...**
15:00	
16:00	
17:00	**Today's self care**
18:00	
19:00	
20:00	**Chart your cycle**
21:00	
22:00	
23:00	**Positive affirmation**
Notes	

Sunday | 28 January 2024 - Waning Gibbous

6:00	**Today's quick wins**
7:00	
8:00	
9:00	
10:00	
11:00	**Health and nutrition**
12:00	
13:00	
14:00	**Today, I am grateful for...**
15:00	
16:00	
17:00	**Today's self care**
18:00	
19:00	
20:00	**Chart your cycle**
21:00	
22:00	
23:00	**Positive affirmation**

Notes

Monday | 29 January 2024 - Waning Gibbous

6:00	**Today's quick wins**
7:00	
8:00	
9:00	
10:00	
11:00	**Health and nutrition**
12:00	
13:00	
14:00	**Today, I am grateful for...**
15:00	
16:00	
17:00	**Today's self care**
18:00	
19:00	
20:00	**Chart your cycle**
21:00	
22:00	
23:00	**Positive affirmation**
Notes	

Tuesday | 30 January 2024 - Waning Gibbous

6:00	**Today's quick wins**
7:00	
8:00	
9:00	
10:00	
11:00	**Health and nutrition**
12:00	
13:00	
14:00	**Today, I am grateful for...**
15:00	
16:00	
17:00	**Today's self care**
18:00	
19:00	
20:00	**Chart your cycle**
21:00	
22:00	
23:00	**Positive affirmation**

Notes

Wednesday | 31 January 2024 - Waning Gibbous

6:00		Today's quick wins	
7:00			
8:00			
9:00			
10:00			
11:00		Health and nutrition	
12:00			
13:00			
14:00		Today, I am grateful for...	
15:00			
16:00			
17:00		Today's self care	
18:00			
19:00			
20:00		Chart your cycle	
21:00			
22:00			
23:00		Positive affirmation	

Notes

January achievements

Be proud of yourself and all that you have achieved this month. Write down your wins, big and small. If you have not achieved everything that you set out to do, that's okay! We learn and grow through our mistakes and experiences. You can use this space to make notes about anything that you have learned.

February 2024

Notes	Monday	Tuesday	Wednesday
	5	6	7
	12	13	14
	19	20	21
	26	27	28

Thursday	Friday	Saturday	Sunday
1	2	3	4
8	9	10	11
15	16	17	18
22	23	24	25
29	1	2	3

February
Godess Asase Yaa

ASASE YAA

West African goddess of the Earth, truth and peace.

The indigenous Akan people of Ghana believe the Earth is a female spirit who is known as Asase Yaa. The Akan connect with their ancestors by dancing and calling out Asase's name. During funeral rites Asase is looked to for protection.

She has no temples, people honour her by protecting and honouring Earth.

She is the upholder of truth. In parts of Ghana if someone is suspected of telling a lie, they are dared to touch the Earth with their tongue to prove they are being honest. On Thursdays, the day of Asase's birth, farmers take a break to give Earth a rest. We must also give Earth a rest and bare her in mind when we make every day decisions such as sourcing our food, limiting plastic purchases and eliminating pesticides from our gardens.

Book: Heal Thyself by Queens Afua
Song: We Will Not Be Silenced by Olivia Fern
Moon phase: Crescent moon
Crystal: Smoky Quartz

My Vision for February

"Our deepest fear is not that we are inadequate. Our deepest fear is that we are powerful beyond measure. It is our light, not our darkness that most frightens us. We ask ourselves, 'Who am I ww\$to be brilliant, gorgeous, talented, fabulous?' Actually, who are you not to be? Your playing small does not serve the world."

– Marianne Williamson

We tend to be more fearful of success than we are of failure. Is there any area in life where you are stopping yourself from achieving greatness in order to protect yourself?

Thursday | 1 February 2024 - Waning Gibbous

6:00	**Today's quick wins**
7:00	
8:00	
9:00	
10:00	
11:00	**Health and nutrition**
12:00	
13:00	
14:00	**Today, I am grateful for...**
15:00	
16:00	
17:00	**Today's self care**
18:00	
19:00	
20:00	**Chart your cycle**
21:00	
22:00	
23:00	**Positive affirmation**

Notes

Friday | 2 February 2024 - Last Quarter

6:00		Today's quick wins
7:00		
8:00		
9:00		
10:00		
11:00		Health and nutrition
12:00		
13:00		
14:00		Today, I am grateful for...
15:00		
16:00		
17:00		Today's self care
18:00		
19:00		
20:00		Chart your cycle
21:00		
22:00		
23:00		Positive affirmation

Notes

Saturday | 3 February 2024 - Last Quarter

6:00	**Today's quick wins**
7:00	
8:00	
9:00	
10:00	
11:00	**Health and nutrition**
12:00	
13:00	
14:00	**Today, I am grateful for...**
15:00	
16:00	
17:00	**Today's self care**
18:00	
19:00	
20:00	**Chart your cycle**
21:00	
22:00	
23:00	**Positive affirmation**
Notes	

Sunday | 4 February 2024 - Waning Crescent

6:00	**Today's quick wins**
7:00	
8:00	
9:00	
10:00	
11:00	**Health and nutrition**
12:00	
13:00	
14:00	**Today, I am grateful for...**
15:00	
16:00	
17:00	**Today's self care**
18:00	
19:00	
20:00	**Chart your cycle**
21:00	
22:00	
23:00	**Positive affirmation**

Notes

Monday | 5 February 2024 - Waning Crescent

6:00	**Today's quick wins**
7:00	
8:00	
9:00	
10:00	
11:00	**Health and nutrition**
12:00	
13:00	
14:00	**Today, I am grateful for...**
15:00	
16:00	
17:00	**Today's self care**
18:00	
19:00	
20:00	**Chart your cycle**
21:00	
22:00	
23:00	**Positive affirmation**
Notes	

Tuesday | 6 February 2024 - Waning Crescent

6:00	Today's quick wins	
7:00		
8:00		
9:00		
10:00		
11:00	Health and nutrition	
12:00		
13:00		
14:00	Today, I am grateful for...	
15:00		
16:00		
17:00	Today's self care	
18:00		
19:00		
20:00	Chart your cycle	
21:00		
22:00		
23:00	Positive affirmation	

Notes

Wednesday | 7 February 2024 - Waning Crescent

6:00	**Today's quick wins**
7:00	
8:00	
9:00	
10:00	
11:00	**Health and nutrition**
12:00	
13:00	
14:00	**Today, I am grateful for...**
15:00	
16:00	
17:00	**Today's self care**
18:00	
19:00	
20:00	**Chart your cycle**
21:00	
22:00	
23:00	**Positive affirmation**
Notes	

Thursday | 8 February 2024 - Waning Crescent

6:00		**Today's quick wins**	
7:00			
8:00			
9:00			
10:00			
11:00		**Health and nutrition**	
12:00			
13:00			
14:00		**Today, I am grateful for...**	
15:00			
16:00			
17:00		**Today's self care**	
18:00			
19:00			
20:00		**Chart your cycle**	
21:00			
22:00			
23:00		**Positive affirmation**	

Notes

Friday | 9 February 2024 - New Moon in Aquarius 22.58 GMT

6:00	**Today's quick wins**
7:00	
8:00	
9:00	
10:00	
11:00	**Health and nutrition**
12:00	
13:00	
14:00	**Today, I am grateful for...**
15:00	
16:00	
17:00	**Today's self care**
18:00	
19:00	
20:00	**Chart your cycle**
21:00	
22:00	
23:00	**Positive affirmation**
Notes	

Saturday | 10 February 2024 - Waxing Cresecent

6:00	**Today's quick wins**
7:00	
8:00	
9:00	
10:00	
11:00	**Health and nutrition**
12:00	
13:00	
14:00	**Today, I am grateful for...**
15:00	
16:00	
17:00	**Today's self care**
18:00	
19:00	
20:00	**Chart your cycle**
21:00	
22:00	
23:00	**Positive affirmation**

Notes

Sunday | 11 February 2024 - Waxing Cresecent

6:00	**Today's quick wins**
7:00	
8:00	
9:00	
10:00	
11:00	**Health and nutrition**
12:00	
13:00	
14:00	**Today, I am grateful for...**
15:00	
16:00	
17:00	**Today's self care**
18:00	
19:00	
20:00	**Chart your cycle**
21:00	
22:00	
23:00	**Positive affirmation**
Notes	

Monday | 12 February 2024 - Waxing Cresecent

6:00	**Today's quick wins**
7:00	
8:00	
9:00	
10:00	
11:00	**Health and nutrition**
12:00	
13:00	
14:00	**Today, I am grateful for...**
15:00	
16:00	
17:00	**Today's self care**
18:00	
19:00	
20:00	**Chart your cycle**
21:00	
22:00	
23:00	**Positive affirmation**

Notes

Tuesday | 13 February 2024 - Waxing Cresecent

6:00	**Today's quick wins**
7:00	
8:00	
9:00	
10:00	
11:00	**Health and nutrition**
12:00	
13:00	
14:00	**Today, I am grateful for...**
15:00	
16:00	
17:00	**Today's self care**
18:00	
19:00	
20:00	**Chart your cycle**
21:00	
22:00	
23:00	**Positive affirmation**

Notes

Wednesday | 14 February 2024 - Waxing Cresecent

6:00	**Today's quick wins**
7:00	
8:00	
9:00	
10:00	
11:00	**Health and nutrition**
12:00	
13:00	
14:00	**Today, I am grateful for...**
15:00	
16:00	
17:00	**Today's self care**
18:00	
19:00	
20:00	**Chart your cycle**
21:00	
22:00	
23:00	**Positive affirmation**

Notes

Thursday | 15 January 2024 - Waxing Cresecent

6:00	**Today's quick wins**
7:00	
8:00	
9:00	
10:00	
11:00	**Health and nutrition**
12:00	
13:00	
14:00	**Today, I am grateful for...**
15:00	
16:00	
17:00	**Today's self care**
18:00	
19:00	
20:00	**Chart your cycle**
21:00	
22:00	
23:00	**Positive affirmation**
Notes	

Friday | 16 February 2024 - First Quarter

6:00		Today's quick wins
7:00		
8:00		
9:00		
10:00		
11:00		Health and nutrition
12:00		
13:00		
14:00		Today, I am grateful for...
15:00		
16:00		
17:00		Today's self care
18:00		
19:00		
20:00		Chart your cycle
21:00		
22:00		
23:00		Positive affirmation
Notes		

Saturday | 17 February 2024 - Waxing Gibbous

6:00	**Today's quick wins**
7:00	
8:00	
9:00	
10:00	
11:00	**Health and nutrition**
12:00	
13:00	
14:00	**Today, I am grateful for...**
15:00	
16:00	
17:00	**Today's self care**
18:00	
19:00	
20:00	**Chart your cycle**
21:00	
22:00	
23:00	**Positive affirmation**

Notes

Sunday | 18 February 2024 - Waxing Gibbous

6:00	**Today's quick wins**
7:00	
8:00	
9:00	
10:00	
11:00	**Health and nutrition**
12:00	
13:00	
14:00	**Today, I am grateful for...**
15:00	
16:00	
17:00	**Today's self care**
18:00	
19:00	
20:00	**Chart your cycle**
21:00	
22:00	
23:00	**Positive affirmation**

Notes

Monday | 19 February 2024 - Waxing Gibbous

6:00		Today's quick wins	
7:00			
8:00			
9:00			
10:00			
11:00		Health and nutrition	
12:00			
13:00			
14:00		Today, I am grateful for...	
15:00			
16:00			
17:00		Today's self care	
18:00			
19:00			
20:00		Chart your cycle	
21:00			
22:00			
23:00		Positive affirmation	
Notes			

Tuesday | 20 February 2024 - Waxing Gibbous

6:00		**Today's quick wins**
7:00		
8:00		
9:00		
10:00		
11:00		**Health and nutrition**
12:00		
13:00		
14:00		**Today, I am grateful for...**
15:00		
16:00		
17:00		**Today's self care**
18:00		
19:00		
20:00		**Chart your cycle**
21:00		
22:00		
23:00		**Positive affirmation**

Notes

Wednesday | 21 February 2024 - Waxing Gibbous

6:00	**Today's quick wins**
7:00	
8:00	
9:00	
10:00	
11:00	**Health and nutrition**
12:00	
13:00	
14:00	**Today, I am grateful for...**
15:00	
16:00	
17:00	**Today's self care**
18:00	
19:00	
20:00	**Chart your cycle**
21:00	
22:00	
23:00	**Positive affirmation**
Notes	

Thursday | 22 February 2024 - Waxing Gibbous

6:00		Today's quick wins
7:00		
8:00		
9:00		
10:00		
11:00		Health and nutrition
12:00		
13:00		
14:00		Today, I am grateful for...
15:00		
16:00		
17:00		Today's self care
18:00		
19:00		
20:00		Chart your cycle
21:00		
22:00		
23:00		Positive affirmation
Notes		

Friday | 23 February 2024 - Waxing Gibbous

6:00	**Today's quick wins**
7:00	
8:00	
9:00	
10:00	
11:00	**Health and nutrition**
12:00	
13:00	
14:00	**Today, I am grateful for...**
15:00	
16:00	
17:00	**Today's self care**
18:00	
19:00	
20:00	**Chart your cycle**
21:00	
22:00	
23:00	**Positive affirmation**
Notes	

Saturday | 24 February 2024 - Full Moon in Virgo 12.30 GMT

6:00	Today's quick wins
7:00	
8:00	
9:00	
10:00	
11:00	Health and nutrition
12:00	
13:00	
14:00	Today, I am grateful for...
15:00	
16:00	
17:00	Today's self care
18:00	
19:00	
20:00	Chart your cycle
21:00	
22:00	
23:00	Positive affirmation

Notes

Sunday | 25 February 2024 - Waning Gibbous

6:00	**Today's quick wins**
7:00	
8:00	
9:00	
10:00	
11:00	**Health and nutrition**
12:00	
13:00	
14:00	**Today, I am grateful for...**
15:00	
16:00	
17:00	**Today's self care**
18:00	
19:00	
20:00	**Chart your cycle**
21:00	
22:00	
23:00	**Positive affirmation**

Notes

Monday | 26 February 2024 - Waning Gibbous

6:00	Today's quick wins	
7:00		
8:00		
9:00		
10:00		
11:00	Health and nutrition	
12:00		
13:00		
14:00	Today, I am grateful for...	
15:00		
16:00		
17:00	Today's self care	
18:00		
19:00		
20:00	Chart your cycle	
21:00		
22:00		
23:00	Positive affirmation	
Notes		

Tuesday | 27 February 2024 - Waning Gibbous

6:00	**Today's quick wins**
7:00	
8:00	
9:00	
10:00	
11:00	**Health and nutrition**
12:00	
13:00	
14:00	**Today, I am grateful for...**
15:00	
16:00	
17:00	**Today's self care**
18:00	
19:00	
20:00	**Chart your cycle**
21:00	
22:00	
23:00	**Positive affirmation**

Notes

Wednesday | 28 February 2024 - Waning Gibbous

6:00	**Today's quick wins**
7:00	
8:00	
9:00	
10:00	
11:00	**Health and nutrition**
12:00	
13:00	
14:00	**Today, I am grateful for...**
15:00	
16:00	
17:00	**Today's self care**
18:00	
19:00	
20:00	**Chart your cycle**
21:00	
22:00	
23:00	**Positive affirmation**

Notes

Thursday | 29 February 2024 - Waning Gibbous

6:00	**Today's quick wins**
7:00	
8:00	
9:00	
10:00	
11:00	**Health and nutrition**
12:00	
13:00	
14:00	**Today, I am grateful for...**
15:00	
16:00	
17:00	**Today's self care**
18:00	
19:00	
20:00	**Chart your cycle**
21:00	
22:00	
23:00	**Positive affirmation**
Notes	

"Our beliefs are like unquestioned commands, telling us how things are, what's possible and impossible and what we can and can not do. They shape every action, every thought, and every feeling that we experience. As a result, changing our belief systems is central to making any real and lasting change in our lives."

– Tony Robbins

February achievements

Be proud of yourself and all that you have achieved this month. Write down your wins, big and small. If you have not achieved everything that you set out to do, that's okay! We learn and grow through our mistakes and experiences. You can use this space to make notes about anything that you have learned.

March 2024

Notes	Monday	Tuesday	Wednesday
	4	5	6
	11	12	13
	18	19	20 *Spring Equinox*
	25 ○	26	27

Thursday	Friday	Saturday	Sunday
29	1	2	3
7	8	9	10
14	15	16	17
21	22	23	24
28	29	30	31

March
Spider Mother

SPIDER MOTHER

Wise, kind protector.

In Hopi legends she represents the web that binds us all together. In times of polarisation when the world feels heavy we can look to Spider mother weaving her web of connection between us all.

A thread that connects us to nature, animals and each other.

In some stories she provides chants of protection. We too can take her lead by writing down some protective or healing mantras to calm our nervous systems in times of stress.

Book: Rainbow Medicine by Wolf Moondance
Song: Grandmother Song by Sheffy Oren Bach
Moon phase: New moon
Crystal: Garnet

My Vision for March

Friday | 1 March 2024 - Waning Gibbous

6:00		**Today's quick wins**	
7:00			
8:00			
9:00			
10:00			
11:00		**Health and nutrition**	
12:00			
13:00			
14:00		**Today, I am grateful for...**	
15:00			
16:00			
17:00		**Today's self care**	
18:00			
19:00			
20:00		**Chart your cycle**	
21:00			
22:00			
23:00		**Positive affirmation**	

Notes

Saturday | 2 March 2024 - Waning Gibbous

6:00	**Today's quick wins**
7:00	
8:00	
9:00	
10:00	
11:00	**Health and nutrition**
12:00	
13:00	
14:00	**Today, I am grateful for...**
15:00	
16:00	
17:00	**Today's self care**
18:00	
19:00	
20:00	**Chart your cycle**
21:00	
22:00	
23:00	**Positive affirmation**
Notes	

Sunday | 3 March 2024 - Last Quarter

6:00		Today's quick wins	
7:00			
8:00			
9:00			
10:00			
11:00		Health and nutrition	
12:00			
13:00			
14:00		Today, I am grateful for...	
15:00			
16:00			
17:00		Today's self care	
18:00			
19:00			
20:00		Chart your cycle	
21:00			
22:00			
23:00		Positive affirmation	

Notes

Monday | 4 March 2024 - Waning Crescent

6:00		Today's quick wins
7:00		
8:00		
9:00		
10:00		
11:00		Health and nutrition
12:00		
13:00		
14:00		Today, I am grateful for...
15:00		
16:00		
17:00		Today's self care
18:00		
19:00		
20:00		Chart your cycle
21:00		
22:00		
23:00		Positive affirmation

Notes

Tuesday | 5 March 2024 - Waning Crescent

6:00		Today's quick wins	
7:00			
8:00			
9:00			
10:00			
11:00		Health and nutrition	
12:00			
13:00			
14:00		Today, I am grateful for...	
15:00			
16:00			
17:00		Today's self care	
18:00			
19:00			
20:00		Chart your cycle	
21:00			
22:00			
23:00		Positive affirmation	

Notes

Wednesday | 6 March 2024 - Waning Crescent

6:00		**Today's quick wins**
7:00		
8:00		
9:00		
10:00		
11:00		**Health and nutrition**
12:00		
13:00		
14:00		**Today, I am grateful for...**
15:00		
16:00		
17:00		**Today's self care**
18:00		
19:00		
20:00		**Chart your cycle**
21:00		
22:00		
23:00		**Positive affirmation**

Notes

Thursday | 7 March 2024 - Waning Crescent

6:00	**Today's quick wins**
7:00	
8:00	
9:00	
10:00	
11:00	**Health and nutrition**
12:00	
13:00	
14:00	**Today, I am grateful for...**
15:00	
16:00	
17:00	**Today's self care**
18:00	
19:00	
20:00	**Chart your cycle**
21:00	
22:00	
23:00	**Positive affirmation**

Notes

Friday | 8 March 2024 - Waning Crescent

6:00		**Today's quick wins**	
7:00			
8:00			
9:00			
10:00			
11:00		**Health and nutrition**	
12:00			
13:00			
14:00		**Today, I am grateful for...**	
15:00			
16:00			
17:00		**Today's self care**	
18:00			
19:00			
20:00		**Chart your cycle**	
21:00			
22:00			
23:00		**Positive affirmation**	

Notes

Saturday | 9 March 2024 - Waning Crescent

6:00		Today's quick wins	
7:00			
8:00			
9:00			
10:00			
11:00		Health and nutrition	
12:00			
13:00			
14:00		Today, I am grateful for...	
15:00			
16:00			
17:00		Today's self care	
18:00			
19:00			
20:00		Chart your cycle	
21:00			
22:00			
23:00		Positive affirmation	

Notes

Sunday | 10 March 2024 - New Moon in Pisces 09.00 GMT

6:00	**Today's quick wins**
7:00	
8:00	
9:00	
10:00	
11:00	**Health and nutrition**
12:00	
13:00	
14:00	**Today, I am grateful for...**
15:00	
16:00	
17:00	**Today's self care**
18:00	
19:00	
20:00	**Chart your cycle**
21:00	
22:00	
23:00	**Positive affirmation**
Notes	

Monday | 11 March 2024 - Waxing Crescent

6:00		**Today's quick wins**	
7:00			
8:00			
9:00			
10:00			
11:00		**Health and nutrition**	
12:00			
13:00			
14:00		**Today, I am grateful for...**	
15:00			
16:00			
17:00		**Today's self care**	
18:00			
19:00			
20:00		**Chart your cycle**	
21:00			
22:00			
23:00		**Positive affirmation**	

Notes

Tuesday | 12 March 2024 - Waxing Crescent

6:00	**Today's quick wins**
7:00	
8:00	
9:00	
10:00	
11:00	**Health and nutrition**
12:00	
13:00	
14:00	**Today, I am grateful for...**
15:00	
16:00	
17:00	**Today's self care**
18:00	
19:00	
20:00	**Chart your cycle**
21:00	
22:00	
23:00	**Positive affirmation**

Notes

Wednesday | 13 March 2024 - Waxing Crescent

6:00	**Today's quick wins**
7:00	
8:00	
9:00	
10:00	
11:00	**Health and nutrition**
12:00	
13:00	
14:00	**Today, I am grateful for...**
15:00	
16:00	
17:00	**Today's self care**
18:00	
19:00	
20:00	**Chart your cycle**
21:00	
22:00	
23:00	**Positive affirmation**
Notes	

Thursday | 14 March 2024 - Waxing Crescent

6:00	**Today's quick wins**
7:00	
8:00	
9:00	
10:00	
11:00	**Health and nutrition**
12:00	
13:00	
14:00	**Today, I am grateful for...**
15:00	
16:00	
17:00	**Today's self care**
18:00	
19:00	
20:00	**Chart your cycle**
21:00	
22:00	
23:00	**Positive affirmation**

Notes

Friday | 15 March 2024 - Waxing Crescent

6:00		**Today's quick wins**
7:00		
8:00		
9:00		
10:00		
11:00		**Health and nutrition**
12:00		
13:00		
14:00		**Today, I am grateful for...**
15:00		
16:00		
17:00		**Today's self care**
18:00		
19:00		
20:00		**Chart your cycle**
21:00		
22:00		
23:00		**Positive affirmation**
Notes		

Saturday | 16 March 2024 - Waxing Crescent

6:00	**Today's quick wins**
7:00	
8:00	
9:00	
10:00	
11:00	**Health and nutrition**
12:00	
13:00	
14:00	**Today, I am grateful for...**
15:00	
16:00	
17:00	**Today's self care**
18:00	
19:00	
20:00	**Chart your cycle**
21:00	
22:00	
23:00	**Positive affirmation**
Notes	

Sunday | 17 March 2024 - First Quarter

6:00	Today's quick wins	
7:00		
8:00		
9:00		
10:00		
11:00	Health and nutrition	
12:00		
13:00		
14:00	Today, I am grateful for...	
15:00		
16:00		
17:00	Today's self care	
18:00		
19:00		
20:00	Chart your cycle	
21:00		
22:00		
23:00	Positive affirmation	
Notes		

Monday | 18 March 2024 - Waxing Gibbous

6:00	**Today's quick wins**	
7:00		
8:00		
9:00		
10:00		
11:00	**Health and nutrition**	
12:00		
13:00		
14:00	**Today, I am grateful for...**	
15:00		
16:00		
17:00	**Today's self care**	
18:00		
19:00		
20:00	**Chart your cycle**	
21:00		
22:00		
23:00	**Positive affirmation**	
Notes		

Tuesday | 19 March 2024 - Waxing Gibbous

6:00	**Today's quick wins**
7:00	
8:00	
9:00	
10:00	
11:00	**Health and nutrition**
12:00	
13:00	
14:00	**Today, I am grateful for...**
15:00	
16:00	
17:00	**Today's self care**
18:00	
19:00	
20:00	**Chart your cycle**
21:00	
22:00	
23:00	**Positive affirmation**

Notes

Wednesday | 20 March 2024 - Waxing Gibbous

6:00	Today's quick wins	
7:00		
8:00		
9:00		
10:00		
11:00	Health and nutrition	
12:00		
13:00		
14:00	Today, I am grateful for...	
15:00		
16:00		
17:00	Today's self care	
18:00		
19:00		
20:00	Chart your cycle	
21:00		
22:00		
23:00	Positive affirmation	
Notes		

Thursday | 21 March 2024 - Waxing Gibbous

6:00		Today's quick wins
7:00		
8:00		
9:00		
10:00		
11:00		Health and nutrition
12:00		
13:00		
14:00		Today, I am grateful for...
15:00		
16:00		
17:00		Today's self care
18:00		
19:00		
20:00		Chart your cycle
21:00		
22:00		
23:00		Positive affirmation
Notes		

Friday | 22 March 2024 - Waxing Gibbous

6:00	**Today's quick wins**
7:00	
8:00	
9:00	
10:00	
11:00	**Health and nutrition**
12:00	
13:00	
14:00	**Today, I am grateful for...**
15:00	
16:00	
17:00	**Today's self care**
18:00	
19:00	
20:00	**Chart your cycle**
21:00	
22:00	
23:00	**Positive affirmation**

Notes

Saturday | 23 March 2024 - Waxing Gibbous

6:00		**Today's quick wins**
7:00		
8:00		
9:00		
10:00		
11:00		**Health and nutrition**
12:00		
13:00		
14:00		**Today, I am grateful for...**
15:00		
16:00		
17:00		**Today's self care**
18:00		
19:00		
20:00		**Chart your cycle**
21:00		
22:00		
23:00		**Positive affirmation**
Notes		

Sunday | 24 March 2024 - Waxing Gibbous

6:00		**Today's quick wins**
7:00		
8:00		
9:00		
10:00		
11:00		**Health and nutrition**
12:00		
13:00		
14:00		**Today, I am grateful for...**
15:00		
16:00		
17:00		**Today's self care**
18:00		
19:00		
20:00		**Chart your cycle**
21:00		
22:00		
23:00		**Positive affirmation**

Notes

Monday | 25 March 2024 - Full Moon in Libra Lunar Eclipse 07.00 GMT

6:00	**Today's quick wins**
7:00	
8:00	
9:00	
10:00	
11:00	**Health and nutrition**
12:00	
13:00	
14:00	**Today, I am grateful for...**
15:00	
16:00	
17:00	**Today's self care**
18:00	
19:00	
20:00	**Chart your cycle**
21:00	
22:00	
23:00	**Positive affirmation**

Notes

Tuesday | 26 March 2024 - Waning Gibbous

6:00	**Today's quick wins**
7:00	
8:00	
9:00	
10:00	
11:00	**Health and nutrition**
12:00	
13:00	
14:00	**Today, I am grateful for...**
15:00	
16:00	
17:00	**Today's self care**
18:00	
19:00	
20:00	**Chart your cycle**
21:00	
22:00	
23:00	**Positive affirmation**

Notes

Wednesday | 27 March 2024 - Waning Gibbous

6:00		Today's quick wins	
7:00			
8:00			
9:00			
10:00			
11:00		Health and nutrition	
12:00			
13:00			
14:00		Today, I am grateful for...	
15:00			
16:00			
17:00		Today's self care	
18:00			
19:00			
20:00		Chart your cycle	
21:00			
22:00			
23:00		Positive affirmation	
Notes			

Thursday | 28 March 2024 - Waning Gibbous

6:00	**Today's quick wins**
7:00	
8:00	
9:00	
10:00	
11:00	**Health and nutrition**
12:00	
13:00	
14:00	**Today, I am grateful for...**
15:00	
16:00	
17:00	**Today's self care**
18:00	
19:00	
20:00	**Chart your cycle**
21:00	
22:00	
23:00	**Positive affirmation**

Notes

Friday | 29 March 2024 - Waning Gibbous

6:00	Today's quick wins	
7:00		
8:00		
9:00		
10:00		
11:00	Health and nutrition	
12:00		
13:00		
14:00	Today, I am grateful for...	
15:00		
16:00		
17:00	Today's self care	
18:00		
19:00		
20:00	Chart your cycle	
21:00		
22:00		
23:00	Positive affirmation	
Notes		

Saturday | 30 March 2024 - Waning Gibbous

6:00	**Today's quick wins**
7:00	
8:00	
9:00	
10:00	
11:00	**Health and nutrition**
12:00	
13:00	
14:00	**Today, I am grateful for...**
15:00	
16:00	
17:00	**Today's self care**
18:00	
19:00	
20:00	**Chart your cycle**
21:00	
22:00	
23:00	**Positive affirmation**
Notes	

Sunday | 31 March 2024 - Waning Gibbous

6:00	**Today's quick wins**
7:00	
8:00	
9:00	
10:00	
11:00	**Health and nutrition**
12:00	
13:00	
14:00	**Today, I am grateful for...**
15:00	
16:00	
17:00	**Today's self care**
18:00	
19:00	
20:00	**Chart your cycle**
21:00	
22:00	
23:00	**Positive affirmation**
Notes	

March achievements

Be proud of yourself and all that you have achieved this month. Write down your wins, big and small. If you have not achieved everything that you set out to do, that's okay! We learn and grow through our mistakes and experiences. You can use this space to make notes about anything that you have learned.

April 2024

Notes	Monday	Tuesday	Wednesday
	1	2 ☽	3
	8 ●	9	10
	15 ☾	16	17
	22	23 ○	24
	29	30	

Thursday	Friday	Saturday	Sunday
4	5	6	7
11	12	13	14
18	19	20	21
25	26	27	28
2	3	4	5

VENUS

Roman goddess of love, beauty and devotion.

Her name comes from the latin word for love. She embodies all things beautiful, has a fluid sexuality and is loved by gods and mortals - both men and women.

The guardian of lovers. Her symbols are the rose, sea shells and myrtle. Festivals were held for her in April to welcome in Spring.

She encourages us to lead heart centred lives. We can honour her energy by engaging in heart based practices such as heart chakra meditations and finding the beauty in every day life.

Books: The Mastery of Love by Don Miguel Ruiz
Song: The Planets, Op.32:2. Venus, the bringer of peace by Gustav Holst
Moon phase: Crescent
Crystal: Emerald

My Vision for April

Monday | 1 April 2024 - Waning Gibbous

6:00		Today's quick wins
7:00		
8:00		
9:00		
10:00		
11:00		Health and nutrition
12:00		
13:00		
14:00		Today, I am grateful for...
15:00		
16:00		
17:00		Today's self care
18:00		
19:00		
20:00		Chart your cycle
21:00		
22:00		
23:00		Positive affirmation

Notes

Tuesday | 2 April 2024 - Last Quarter

6:00	**Today's quick wins**
7:00	
8:00	
9:00	
10:00	
11:00	**Health and nutrition**
12:00	
13:00	
14:00	**Today, I am grateful for...**
15:00	
16:00	
17:00	**Today's self care**
18:00	
19:00	
20:00	**Chart your cycle**
21:00	
22:00	
23:00	**Positive affirmation**

Notes

Wednesday | 3 April 2024 - Waning Crescent

6:00		Today's quick wins	
7:00			
8:00			
9:00			
10:00			
11:00		Health and nutrition	
12:00			
13:00			
14:00		Today, I am grateful for...	
15:00			
16:00			
17:00		Today's self care	
18:00			
19:00			
20:00		Chart your cycle	
21:00			
22:00			
23:00		Positive affirmation	
Notes			

Thursday | 4 April 2024 - Waning Crescent

6:00	**Today's quick wins**
7:00	
8:00	
9:00	
10:00	
11:00	**Health and nutrition**
12:00	
13:00	
14:00	**Today, I am grateful for...**
15:00	
16:00	
17:00	**Today's self care**
18:00	
19:00	
20:00	**Chart your cycle**
21:00	
22:00	
23:00	**Positive affirmation**
Notes	

Friday | 5 April 2024 - Waning Crescent

6:00		Today's quick wins
7:00		
8:00		
9:00		
10:00		
11:00		Health and nutrition
12:00		
13:00		
14:00		Today, I am grateful for...
15:00		
16:00		
17:00		Today's self care
18:00		
19:00		
20:00		Chart your cycle
21:00		
22:00		
23:00		Positive affirmation

Notes

Saturday | 6 April 2024 - Waning Crescent

6:00	**Today's quick wins**
7:00	
8:00	
9:00	
10:00	
11:00	**Health and nutrition**
12:00	
13:00	
14:00	**Today, I am grateful for...**
15:00	
16:00	
17:00	**Today's self care**
18:00	
19:00	
20:00	**Chart your cycle**
21:00	
22:00	
23:00	**Positive affirmation**

Notes

Sunday | 7 April 2024 - Waning Crescent

6:00		Today's quick wins
7:00		
8:00		
9:00		
10:00		
11:00		Health and nutrition
12:00		
13:00		
14:00		Today, I am grateful for...
15:00		
16:00		
17:00		Today's self care
18:00		
19:00		
20:00		Chart your cycle
21:00		
22:00		
23:00		Positive affirmation

Notes

Monday | 8 April 2024 - New Moon in Aries Solar Eclipse 18.20 GMT

6:00	**Today's quick wins**
7:00	
8:00	
9:00	
10:00	
11:00	**Health and nutrition**
12:00	
13:00	
14:00	**Today, I am grateful for...**
15:00	
16:00	
17:00	**Today's self care**
18:00	
19:00	
20:00	**Chart your cycle**
21:00	
22:00	
23:00	**Positive affirmation**
Notes	

Tuesday | 9 April 2024 - Waxing Crescent

6:00		**Today's quick wins**	
7:00			
8:00			
9:00			
10:00			
11:00		**Health and nutrition**	
12:00			
13:00			
14:00		**Today, I am grateful for...**	
15:00			
16:00			
17:00		**Today's self care**	
18:00			
19:00			
20:00		**Chart your cycle**	
21:00			
22:00			
23:00		**Positive affirmation**	
Notes			

Wednesday | 10 April 2024 - Waxing Crescent

6:00	**Today's quick wins**
7:00	
8:00	
9:00	
10:00	
11:00	**Health and nutrition**
12:00	
13:00	
14:00	**Today, I am grateful for...**
15:00	
16:00	
17:00	**Today's self care**
18:00	
19:00	
20:00	**Chart your cycle**
21:00	
22:00	
23:00	**Positive affirmation**

Notes

Thursday | 11 April 2024 - Waxing Crescent

6:00	**Today's quick wins**
7:00	
8:00	
9:00	
10:00	
11:00	**Health and nutrition**
12:00	
13:00	
14:00	**Today, I am grateful for...**
15:00	
16:00	
17:00	**Today's self care**
18:00	
19:00	
20:00	**Chart your cycle**
21:00	
22:00	
23:00	**Positive affirmation**
Notes	

Friday | 12 April 2024 - Waxing Crescent

6:00	**Today's quick wins**
7:00	
8:00	
9:00	
10:00	
11:00	**Health and nutrition**
12:00	
13:00	
14:00	**Today, I am grateful for...**
15:00	
16:00	
17:00	**Today's self care**
18:00	
19:00	
20:00	**Chart your cycle**
21:00	
22:00	
23:00	**Positive affirmation**

Notes

Saturday | 13 April 2024 - Waxing Crescent

6:00	**Today's quick wins**
7:00	
8:00	
9:00	
10:00	
11:00	**Health and nutrition**
12:00	
13:00	
14:00	**Today, I am grateful for...**
15:00	
16:00	
17:00	**Today's self care**
18:00	
19:00	
20:00	**Chart your cycle**
21:00	
22:00	
23:00	**Positive affirmation**

Notes

Sunday | 14 April 2024 - Waxing Crescent

6:00	**Today's quick wins**
7:00	
8:00	
9:00	
10:00	
11:00	**Health and nutrition**
12:00	
13:00	
14:00	**Today, I am grateful for...**
15:00	
16:00	
17:00	**Today's self care**
18:00	
19:00	
20:00	**Chart your cycle**
21:00	
22:00	
23:00	**Positive affirmation**

Notes

Monday | 15 April 2024 - First Quarter

6:00	Today's quick wins	
7:00		
8:00		
9:00		
10:00		
11:00	Health and nutrition	
12:00		
13:00		
14:00	Today, I am grateful for…	
15:00		
16:00		
17:00	Today's self care	
18:00		
19:00		
20:00	Chart your cycle	
21:00		
22:00		
23:00	Positive affirmation	
Notes		

Tuesday | 16 April 2024 - Waxing Gibbous

6:00	**Today's quick wins**
7:00	
8:00	
9:00	
10:00	
11:00	**Health and nutrition**
12:00	
13:00	
14:00	**Today, I am grateful for...**
15:00	
16:00	
17:00	**Today's self care**
18:00	
19:00	
20:00	**Chart your cycle**
21:00	
22:00	
23:00	**Positive affirmation**
Notes	

Wednesday | 17 April 2024 - Waxing Gibbous

6:00		**Today's quick wins**
7:00		
8:00		
9:00		
10:00		
11:00		**Health and nutrition**
12:00		
13:00		
14:00		**Today, I am grateful for...**
15:00		
16:00		
17:00		**Today's self care**
18:00		
19:00		
20:00		**Chart your cycle**
21:00		
22:00		
23:00		**Positive affirmation**
Notes		

Thursday | 18 April 2024 - Waxing Gibbous

6:00	**Today's quick wins**
7:00	
8:00	
9:00	
10:00	
11:00	**Health and nutrition**
12:00	
13:00	
14:00	**Today, I am grateful for...**
15:00	
16:00	
17:00	**Today's self care**
18:00	
19:00	
20:00	**Chart your cycle**
21:00	
22:00	
23:00	**Positive affirmation**

Notes

Friday | 19 April 2024 - Waxing Gibbous

6:00		**Today's quick wins**	
7:00			
8:00			
9:00			
10:00			
11:00		**Health and nutrition**	
12:00			
13:00			
14:00		**Today, I am grateful for...**	
15:00			
16:00			
17:00		**Today's self care**	
18:00			
19:00			
20:00		**Chart your cycle**	
21:00			
22:00			
23:00		**Positive affirmation**	

Notes

Saturday | 20 April 2024 - Waxing Gibbous

6:00	**Today's quick wins**
7:00	
8:00	
9:00	
10:00	
11:00	**Health and nutrition**
12:00	
13:00	
14:00	**Today, I am grateful for...**
15:00	
16:00	
17:00	**Today's self care**
18:00	
19:00	
20:00	**Chart your cycle**
21:00	
22:00	
23:00	**Positive affirmation**
Notes	

Sunday | 21 April 2024 - Waxing Gibbous

6:00	Today's quick wins	
7:00		
8:00		
9:00		
10:00		
11:00	Health and nutrition	
12:00		
13:00		
14:00	Today, I am grateful for...	
15:00		
16:00		
17:00	Today's self care	
18:00		
19:00		
20:00	Chart your cycle	
21:00		
22:00		
23:00	Positive affirmation	
Notes		

Monday | 22 April 2024 - Waxing Gibbous

6:00	**Today's quick wins**
7:00	
8:00	
9:00	
10:00	
11:00	**Health and nutrition**
12:00	
13:00	
14:00	**Today, I am grateful for…**
15:00	
16:00	
17:00	**Today's self care**
18:00	
19:00	
20:00	**Chart your cycle**
21:00	
22:00	
23:00	**Positive affirmation**
Notes	

Tuesday | 23 April 2024 - Full Moon in Scorpio 23.48 GMT

6:00		Today's quick wins
7:00		
8:00		
9:00		
10:00		
11:00		Health and nutrition
12:00		
13:00		
14:00		Today, I am grateful for...
15:00		
16:00		
17:00		Today's self care
18:00		
19:00		
20:00		Chart your cycle
21:00		
22:00		
23:00		Positive affirmation
Notes		

# Wednesday | 24 April 2024 - Waning Gibbous

6:00	**Today's quick wins**
7:00	
8:00	
9:00	
10:00	
11:00	**Health and nutrition**
12:00	
13:00	
14:00	**Today, I am grateful for...**
15:00	
16:00	
17:00	**Today's self care**
18:00	
19:00	
20:00	**Chart your cycle**
21:00	
22:00	
23:00	**Positive affirmation**

Notes

Thursday | 25 April 2024 - Waning Gibbous

6:00		Today's quick wins
7:00		
8:00		
9:00		
10:00		
11:00		Health and nutrition
12:00		
13:00		
14:00		Today, I am grateful for...
15:00		
16:00		
17:00		Today's self care
18:00		
19:00		
20:00		Chart your cycle
21:00		
22:00		
23:00		Positive affirmation
Notes		

Friday | 26 April 2024 - Waning Gibbous

6:00		Today's quick wins	
7:00			
8:00			
9:00			
10:00			
11:00		Health and nutrition	
12:00			
13:00			
14:00		Today, I am grateful for...	
15:00			
16:00			
17:00		Today's self care	
18:00			
19:00			
20:00		Chart your cycle	
21:00			
22:00			
23:00		Positive affirmation	
Notes			

Saturday | 27 April 2024 - Waning Gibbous

6:00	**Today's quick wins**
7:00	
8:00	
9:00	
10:00	
11:00	**Health and nutrition**
12:00	
13:00	
14:00	**Today, I am grateful for...**
15:00	
16:00	
17:00	**Today's self care**
18:00	
19:00	
20:00	**Chart your cycle**
21:00	
22:00	
23:00	**Positive affirmation**
Notes	

Sunday | 28 April 2024 - Waning Gibbous

6:00	**Today's quick wins**
7:00	
8:00	
9:00	
10:00	
11:00	**Health and nutrition**
12:00	
13:00	
14:00	**Today, I am grateful for...**
15:00	
16:00	
17:00	**Today's self care**
18:00	
19:00	
20:00	**Chart your cycle**
21:00	
22:00	
23:00	**Positive affirmation**

Notes

Monday | 29 April 2024 - Waning Gibbous

6:00		Today's quick wins
7:00		
8:00		
9:00		
10:00		
11:00		Health and nutrition
12:00		
13:00		
14:00		Today, I am grateful for…
15:00		
16:00		
17:00		Today's self care
18:00		
19:00		
20:00		Chart your cycle
21:00		
22:00		
23:00		Positive affirmation
Notes		

Tuesday | 30 April 2024 - Waning Gibbous

6:00	**Today's quick wins**
7:00	
8:00	
9:00	
10:00	
11:00	**Health and nutrition**
12:00	
13:00	
14:00	**Today, I am grateful for...**
15:00	
16:00	
17:00	**Today's self care**
18:00	
19:00	
20:00	**Chart your cycle**
21:00	
22:00	
23:00	**Positive affirmation**

Notes

April achievements

Be proud of yourself and all that you have achieved this month. Write down your wins, big and small. If you have not achieved everything that you set out to do, that's okay! We learn and grow through our mistakes and experiences. You can use this space to make notes about anything that you have learned.

'We dont see things as they are; We see them as we are'
—Anaïs Nin

May 2024

Notes	Monday	Tuesday	Wednesday
			1
	6	7	8
	13	14	15
	20	21	22
	27	28	29

Thursday	Friday	Saturday	Sunday
2	3	4	5
9	10	11	12
16	17	18	19
23 ○	24	25	26
30	31	1	2

May
Goddess Mazu

MAZU

Chinese goddess of the sea.

It is believed that Mazu lived in tenth century China. She is said to have saved many people lost at sea and she is still a big part of life in coastal areas.

She is celebrated on the 1st of May in Taiwan where locals gather for a Mazu pilgrimage. Ceremonies also take place throughout the year in over 5,000 Mazuz temples where she is honoured with candles, incense and floral tributes.

Books: Wood Becomes Water: Chinese Medicine in Everyday Life by Gail Reichstein
Songs: Jasmine Flower by Lei Qiang
Crystal: Shiva Lingam
Moon phase: Full moon

My Vision for May

Wednesday | 1 May 2024 - Last Quarter

6:00		Today's quick wins
7:00		
8:00		
9:00		
10:00		
11:00		Health and nutrition
12:00		
13:00		
14:00		Today, I am grateful for...
15:00		
16:00		
17:00		Today's self care
18:00		
19:00		
20:00		Chart your cycle
21:00		
22:00		
23:00		Positive affirmation

Notes

Thursday | 2 May 2024 - Waning Crescent

6:00	**Today's quick wins**
7:00	
8:00	
9:00	
10:00	
11:00	**Health and nutrition**
12:00	
13:00	
14:00	**Today, I am grateful for...**
15:00	
16:00	
17:00	**Today's self care**
18:00	
19:00	
20:00	**Chart your cycle**
21:00	
22:00	
23:00	**Positive affirmation**

Notes

Friday | 3 May 2024 - Waning Crescent

6:00		Today's quick wins	
7:00			
8:00			
9:00			
10:00			
11:00		Health and nutrition	
12:00			
13:00			
14:00		Today, I am grateful for...	
15:00			
16:00			
17:00		Today's self care	
18:00			
19:00			
20:00		Chart your cycle	
21:00			
22:00			
23:00		Positive affirmation	
Notes			

Saturday | 4 May 2024 - Waning Crescent

6:00		**Today's quick wins**	
7:00			
8:00			
9:00			
10:00			
11:00		**Health and nutrition**	
12:00			
13:00			
14:00		**Today, I am grateful for...**	
15:00			
16:00			
17:00		**Today's self care**	
18:00			
19:00			
20:00		**Chart your cycle**	
21:00			
22:00			
23:00		**Positive affirmation**	

Notes

Sunday | 5 May 2024 - Waning Crescent

6:00		Today's quick wins
7:00		
8:00		
9:00		
10:00		
11:00		Health and nutrition
12:00		
13:00		
14:00		Today, I am grateful for...
15:00		
16:00		
17:00		Today's self care
18:00		
19:00		
20:00		Chart your cycle
21:00		
22:00		
23:00		Positive affirmation
Notes		

Monday | 6 May 2024 - Waning Crescent

6:00		Today's quick wins
7:00		
8:00		
9:00		
10:00		
11:00		Health and nutrition
12:00		
13:00		
14:00		Today, I am grateful for...
15:00		
16:00		
17:00		Today's self care
18:00		
19:00		
20:00		Chart your cycle
21:00		
22:00		
23:00		Positive affirmation

Notes

Tuesday | 7 May 2024 - Waning Crescent

6:00		Today's quick wins
7:00		
8:00		
9:00		
10:00		
11:00		Health and nutrition
12:00		
13:00		
14:00		Today, I am grateful for…
15:00		
16:00		
17:00		Today's self care
18:00		
19:00		
20:00		Chart your cycle
21:00		
22:00		
23:00		Positive affirmation

Notes

Wednesday | 8 May 2024 - New Moon in Taurus 03.21 GMT

6:00	**Today's quick wins**
7:00	
8:00	
9:00	
10:00	
11:00	**Health and nutrition**
12:00	
13:00	
14:00	**Today, I am grateful for...**
15:00	
16:00	
17:00	**Today's self care**
18:00	
19:00	
20:00	**Chart your cycle**
21:00	
22:00	
23:00	**Positive affirmation**
Notes	

Thursday | 9 May 2024 - Waxing Crescent

6:00		**Today's quick wins**	
7:00			
8:00			
9:00			
10:00			
11:00		**Health and nutrition**	
12:00			
13:00			
14:00		**Today, I am grateful for...**	
15:00			
16:00			
17:00		**Today's self care**	
18:00			
19:00			
20:00		**Chart your cycle**	
21:00			
22:00			
23:00		**Positive affirmation**	

Notes

Friday | 10 May 2024 - Waxing Crescent

6:00	Today's quick wins	
7:00		
8:00		
9:00		
10:00		
11:00	Health and nutrition	
12:00		
13:00		
14:00	Today, I am grateful for…	
15:00		
16:00		
17:00	Today's self care	
18:00		
19:00		
20:00	Chart your cycle	
21:00		
22:00		
23:00	Positive affirmation	

Notes

Saturday | 11 May 2024 - Waxing Crescent

6:00	**Today's quick wins**
7:00	
8:00	
9:00	
10:00	
11:00	**Health and nutrition**
12:00	
13:00	
14:00	**Today, I am grateful for...**
15:00	
16:00	
17:00	**Today's self care**
18:00	
19:00	
20:00	**Chart your cycle**
21:00	
22:00	
23:00	**Positive affirmation**

Notes

Sunday | 12 May 2024 - Waxing Crescent

6:00	**Today's quick wins**
7:00	
8:00	
9:00	
10:00	
11:00	**Health and nutrition**
12:00	
13:00	
14:00	**Today, I am grateful for...**
15:00	
16:00	
17:00	**Today's self care**
18:00	
19:00	
20:00	**Chart your cycle**
21:00	
22:00	
23:00	**Positive affirmation**

Notes

Monday | 13 May 2024 - Waxing Crescent

6:00		Today's quick wins	
7:00			
8:00			
9:00			
10:00			
11:00		Health and nutrition	
12:00			
13:00			
14:00		Today, I am grateful for...	
15:00			
16:00			
17:00		Today's self care	
18:00			
19:00			
20:00		Chart your cycle	
21:00			
22:00			
23:00		Positive affirmation	

Notes

Tuesday | 14 May 2024 - Waxing Crescent

6:00	**Today's quick wins**
7:00	
8:00	
9:00	
10:00	
11:00	**Health and nutrition**
12:00	
13:00	
14:00	**Today, I am grateful for...**
15:00	
16:00	
17:00	**Today's self care**
18:00	
19:00	
20:00	**Chart your cycle**
21:00	
22:00	
23:00	**Positive affirmation**

Notes

Wednesday | 15 May 2024 - First Quarter

6:00		Today's quick wins
7:00		
8:00		
9:00		
10:00		
11:00		Health and nutrition
12:00		
13:00		
14:00		Today, I am grateful for…
15:00		
16:00		
17:00		Today's self care
18:00		
19:00		
20:00		Chart your cycle
21:00		
22:00		
23:00		Positive affirmation

Notes

Thursday | 16 May 2024 - Waxing Gibbous

6:00		**Today's quick wins**	
7:00			
8:00			
9:00			
10:00			
11:00		**Health and nutrition**	
12:00			
13:00			
14:00		**Today, I am grateful for...**	
15:00			
16:00			
17:00		**Today's self care**	
18:00			
19:00			
20:00		**Chart your cycle**	
21:00			
22:00			
23:00		**Positive affirmation**	

Notes

Friday | 17 May 2024 - Waxing Gibbous

6:00		**Today's quick wins**	
7:00			
8:00			
9:00			
10:00			
11:00		**Health and nutrition**	
12:00			
13:00			
14:00		**Today, I am grateful for...**	
15:00			
16:00			
17:00		**Today's self care**	
18:00			
19:00			
20:00		**Chart your cycle**	
21:00			
22:00			
23:00		**Positive affirmation**	

Notes

Saturday | 18 May 2024 - Waxing Gibbous

6:00	**Today's quick wins**
7:00	
8:00	
9:00	
10:00	
11:00	**Health and nutrition**
12:00	
13:00	
14:00	**Today, I am grateful for...**
15:00	
16:00	
17:00	**Today's self care**
18:00	
19:00	
20:00	**Chart your cycle**
21:00	
22:00	
23:00	**Positive affirmation**

Notes

Sunday | 19 May 2024 - Waxing Gibbous

6:00	**Today's quick wins**
7:00	
8:00	
9:00	
10:00	
11:00	**Health and nutrition**
12:00	
13:00	
14:00	**Today, I am grateful for...**
15:00	
16:00	
17:00	**Today's self care**
18:00	
19:00	
20:00	**Chart your cycle**
21:00	
22:00	
23:00	**Positive affirmation**

Notes

Monday | 20 May 2024 - Waxing Gibbous

6:00		**Today's quick wins**	
7:00			
8:00			
9:00			
10:00			
11:00		**Health and nutrition**	
12:00			
13:00			
14:00		**Today, I am grateful for...**	
15:00			
16:00			
17:00		**Today's self care**	
18:00			
19:00			
20:00		**Chart your cycle**	
21:00			
22:00			
23:00		**Positive affirmation**	

Notes

Tuesday | 21 May 2024 - Waxing Gibbous

6:00		Today's quick wins
7:00		
8:00		
9:00		
10:00		
11:00		Health and nutrition
12:00		
13:00		
14:00		Today, I am grateful for...
15:00		
16:00		
17:00		Today's self care
18:00		
19:00		
20:00		Chart your cycle
21:00		
22:00		
23:00		Positive affirmation
Notes		

Wednesday | 22 May 2024 - Waxing Gibbous

6:00		**Today's quick wins**	
7:00			
8:00			
9:00			
10:00			
11:00		**Health and nutrition**	
12:00			
13:00			
14:00		**Today, I am grateful for...**	
15:00			
16:00			
17:00		**Today's self care**	
18:00			
19:00			
20:00		**Chart your cycle**	
21:00			
22:00			
23:00		**Positive affirmation**	
Notes			

Thursday | 23 May 2024 - Full Moon in Sagittarius 13.52 GMT

6:00		Today's quick wins
7:00		
8:00		
9:00		
10:00		
11:00		Health and nutrition
12:00		
13:00		
14:00		Today, I am grateful for...
15:00		
16:00		
17:00		Today's self care
18:00		
19:00		
20:00		Chart your cycle
21:00		
22:00		
23:00		Positive affirmation
Notes		

Friday | 24 May 2024 - Waning Gibbous

6:00	**Today's quick wins**
7:00	
8:00	
9:00	
10:00	
11:00	**Health and nutrition**
12:00	
13:00	
14:00	**Today, I am grateful for...**
15:00	
16:00	
17:00	**Today's self care**
18:00	
19:00	
20:00	**Chart your cycle**
21:00	
22:00	
23:00	**Positive affirmation**

Notes

Saturday | 25 May 2024 - Waning Gibbous

6:00	Today's quick wins
7:00	
8:00	
9:00	
10:00	
11:00	Health and nutrition
12:00	
13:00	
14:00	Today, I am grateful for...
15:00	
16:00	
17:00	Today's self care
18:00	
19:00	
20:00	Chart your cycle
21:00	
22:00	
23:00	Positive affirmation

Notes

Sunday | 26 May 2024 - Waning Gibbous

6:00	**Today's quick wins**
7:00	
8:00	
9:00	
10:00	
11:00	**Health and nutrition**
12:00	
13:00	
14:00	**Today, I am grateful for...**
15:00	
16:00	
17:00	**Today's self care**
18:00	
19:00	
20:00	**Chart your cycle**
21:00	
22:00	
23:00	**Positive affirmation**

Notes

Monday | 27 May 2024 - Waning Gibbous

6:00		**Today's quick wins**	
7:00			
8:00			
9:00			
10:00			
11:00		**Health and nutrition**	
12:00			
13:00			
14:00		**Today, I am grateful for...**	
15:00			
16:00			
17:00		**Today's self care**	
18:00			
19:00			
20:00		**Chart your cycle**	
21:00			
22:00			
23:00		**Positive affirmation**	

Notes

Tuesday | 28 May 2024 - Waning Gibbous

6:00	**Today's quick wins**
7:00	
8:00	
9:00	
10:00	
11:00	**Health and nutrition**
12:00	
13:00	
14:00	**Today, I am grateful for...**
15:00	
16:00	
17:00	**Today's self care**
18:00	
19:00	
20:00	**Chart your cycle**
21:00	
22:00	
23:00	**Positive affirmation**
Notes	

Wednesday | 29 May 2024 - Waning Gibbous

6:00		**Today's quick wins**
7:00		
8:00		
9:00		
10:00		
11:00		**Health and nutrition**
12:00		
13:00		
14:00		**Today, I am grateful for...**
15:00		
16:00		
17:00		**Today's self care**
18:00		
19:00		
20:00		**Chart your cycle**
21:00		
22:00		
23:00		**Positive affirmation**
Notes		

Thursday | 30 May 2024 - Last Quarter

6:00	**Today's quick wins**
7:00	
8:00	
9:00	
10:00	
11:00	**Health and nutrition**
12:00	
13:00	
14:00	**Today, I am grateful for...**
15:00	
16:00	
17:00	**Today's self care**
18:00	
19:00	
20:00	**Chart your cycle**
21:00	
22:00	
23:00	**Positive affirmation**
Notes	

Friday | 31 May 2024 - Waning Crescent

6:00		Today's quick wins
7:00		
8:00		
9:00		
10:00		
11:00		Health and nutrition
12:00		
13:00		
14:00		Today, I am grateful for...
15:00		
16:00		
17:00		Today's self care
18:00		
19:00		
20:00		Chart your cycle
21:00		
22:00		
23:00		Positive affirmation

Notes

May achievements

Be proud of yourself and all that you have achieved this month. Write down your wins, big and small. If you have not achieved everything that you set out to do, that's okay! We learn and grow through our mistakes and experiences. You can use this space to make notes about anything that you have learned.

June 2024

Notes	Monday	Tuesday	Wednesday
	3	4	5
	10	11	12
	17	18	19
	24	25	26

Thursday	Friday	Saturday	Sunday
30	31	1	2
6 ●	7	8	9
13	14 ◐	15	16
20 *Summer Solstice*	21	22 ○	23
27	28 ◗	29	30

June
Goddess Papatuanuku

PAPATUANUKU

Maori Earth goddess.

She is the foundation of all life, source of all things.

Maori tribes view acts of deforestation and the destruction of Earth as an attack on the Goddess. We can all honour Papatuanuku by helping protect our natural world.

We honour her by organising beach clean up days, or joining organisations such as the Rainforest Trust who do some great work and always need support.

Books: Staying Alive by Vandana Shiva
Song: Mother Earth by Karliene
Crystal: Petrified wood
Moon phase: Crescent moon

My Vision for June

Saturday | 1 June 2024 - Waning Crescent

6:00		**Today's quick wins**	
7:00			
8:00			
9:00			
10:00			
11:00		**Health and nutrition**	
12:00			
13:00			
14:00		**Today, I am grateful for...**	
15:00			
16:00			
17:00		**Today's self care**	
18:00			
19:00			
20:00		**Chart your cycle**	
21:00			
22:00			
23:00		**Positive affirmation**	

Notes

Sunday | 2 June 2024 - Waning Crescent

6:00	**Today's quick wins**
7:00	
8:00	
9:00	
10:00	
11:00	**Health and nutrition**
12:00	
13:00	
14:00	**Today, I am grateful for...**
15:00	
16:00	
17:00	**Today's self care**
18:00	
19:00	
20:00	**Chart your cycle**
21:00	
22:00	
23:00	**Positive affirmation**

Notes

Monday | 3 June 2024 - Waning Crescent

6:00		Today's quick wins
7:00		
8:00		
9:00		
10:00		
11:00		Health and nutrition
12:00		
13:00		
14:00		Today, I am grateful for…
15:00		
16:00		
17:00		Today's self care
18:00		
19:00		
20:00		Chart your cycle
21:00		
22:00		
23:00		Positive affirmation

Notes

Tuesday | 4 June 2024 - Waning Crescent

6:00		**Today's quick wins**	
7:00			
8:00			
9:00			
10:00			
11:00		**Health and nutrition**	
12:00			
13:00			
14:00		**Today, I am grateful for...**	
15:00			
16:00			
17:00		**Today's self care**	
18:00			
19:00			
20:00		**Chart your cycle**	
21:00			
22:00			
23:00		**Positive affirmation**	
Notes			

Wednesday | 5 June 2024 - Waning Crescent

6:00		**Today's quick wins**	
7:00			
8:00			
9:00			
10:00			
11:00		**Health and nutrition**	
12:00			
13:00			
14:00		**Today, I am grateful for...**	
15:00			
16:00			
17:00		**Today's self care**	
18:00			
19:00			
20:00		**Chart your cycle**	
21:00			
22:00			
23:00		**Positive affirmation**	

Notes

Thursday | 6 June 2024 - New Moon in Gemini 12.37 GMT

6:00	**Today's quick wins**
7:00	
8:00	
9:00	
10:00	
11:00	**Health and nutrition**
12:00	
13:00	
14:00	**Today, I am grateful for...**
15:00	
16:00	
17:00	**Today's self care**
18:00	
19:00	
20:00	**Chart your cycle**
21:00	
22:00	
23:00	**Positive affirmation**
Notes	

Friday | 7 June 2024 - Waxing Crescent

6:00	**Today's quick wins**
7:00	
8:00	
9:00	
10:00	
11:00	**Health and nutrition**
12:00	
13:00	
14:00	**Today, I am grateful for...**
15:00	
16:00	
17:00	**Today's self care**
18:00	
19:00	
20:00	**Chart your cycle**
21:00	
22:00	
23:00	**Positive affirmation**

Notes

Saturday | 8 June 2024 - Waxing Crescent

6:00	**Today's quick wins**
7:00	
8:00	
9:00	
10:00	
11:00	**Health and nutrition**
12:00	
13:00	
14:00	**Today, I am grateful for...**
15:00	
16:00	
17:00	**Today's self care**
18:00	
19:00	
20:00	**Chart your cycle**
21:00	
22:00	
23:00	**Positive affirmation**

Notes

Sunday | 9 June 2024 - Waxing Crescent

6:00		Today's quick wins
7:00		
8:00		
9:00		
10:00		
11:00		Health and nutrition
12:00		
13:00		
14:00		Today, I am grateful for...
15:00		
16:00		
17:00		Today's self care
18:00		
19:00		
20:00		Chart your cycle
21:00		
22:00		
23:00		Positive affirmation
Notes		

Monday | 10 June 2024 - Waxing Crescent

6:00	**Today's quick wins**
7:00	
8:00	
9:00	
10:00	
11:00	**Health and nutrition**
12:00	
13:00	
14:00	**Today, I am grateful for...**
15:00	
16:00	
17:00	**Today's self care**
18:00	
19:00	
20:00	**Chart your cycle**
21:00	
22:00	
23:00	**Positive affirmation**
Notes	

Tuesday | 11 June 2024 - Waxing Crescent

6:00		**Today's quick wins**
7:00		
8:00		
9:00		
10:00		
11:00		**Health and nutrition**
12:00		
13:00		
14:00		**Today, I am grateful for...**
15:00		
16:00		
17:00		**Today's self care**
18:00		
19:00		
20:00		**Chart your cycle**
21:00		
22:00		
23:00		**Positive affirmation**

Notes

Wednesday | 12 June 2024 - Waxing Crescent

6:00	**Today's quick wins**
7:00	
8:00	
9:00	
10:00	
11:00	**Health and nutrition**
12:00	
13:00	
14:00	**Today, I am grateful for...**
15:00	
16:00	
17:00	**Today's self care**
18:00	
19:00	
20:00	**Chart your cycle**
21:00	
22:00	
23:00	**Positive affirmation**
Notes	

Thursday | 13 June 2024 - Waxing Crescent

6:00		Today's quick wins
7:00		
8:00		
9:00		
10:00		
11:00		Health and nutrition
12:00		
13:00		
14:00		Today, I am grateful for...
15:00		
16:00		
17:00		Today's self care
18:00		
19:00		
20:00		Chart your cycle
21:00		
22:00		
23:00		Positive affirmation
Notes		

Friday | 14 June 2024 - First Quarter

6:00		Today's quick wins
7:00		
8:00		
9:00		
10:00		
11:00		Health and nutrition
12:00		
13:00		
14:00		Today, I am grateful for...
15:00		
16:00		
17:00		Today's self care
18:00		
19:00		
20:00		Chart your cycle
21:00		
22:00		
23:00		Positive affirmation

Notes

# Saturday	15 June 2024 - Waxing Gibbous
6:00	**Today's quick wins**
7:00	
8:00	
9:00	
10:00	
11:00	**Health and nutrition**
12:00	
13:00	
14:00	**Today, I am grateful for...**
15:00	
16:00	
17:00	**Today's self care**
18:00	
19:00	
20:00	**Chart your cycle**
21:00	
22:00	
23:00	**Positive affirmation**
Notes	

Sunday | 16 June 2024 - Waxing Gibbous

6:00	**Today's quick wins**
7:00	
8:00	
9:00	
10:00	
11:00	**Health and nutrition**
12:00	
13:00	
14:00	**Today, I am grateful for...**
15:00	
16:00	
17:00	**Today's self care**
18:00	
19:00	
20:00	**Chart your cycle**
21:00	
22:00	
23:00	**Positive affirmation**
Notes	

Monday | 17 June 2024 - Waxing Gibbous

6:00	**Today's quick wins**
7:00	
8:00	
9:00	
10:00	
11:00	**Health and nutrition**
12:00	
13:00	
14:00	**Today, I am grateful for...**
15:00	
16:00	
17:00	**Today's self care**
18:00	
19:00	
20:00	**Chart your cycle**
21:00	
22:00	
23:00	**Positive affirmation**

Notes

Tuesday | 18 June 2024 - Waxing Gibbous

6:00	**Today's quick wins**
7:00	
8:00	
9:00	
10:00	
11:00	**Health and nutrition**
12:00	
13:00	
14:00	**Today, I am grateful for...**
15:00	
16:00	
17:00	**Today's self care**
18:00	
19:00	
20:00	**Chart your cycle**
21:00	
22:00	
23:00	**Positive affirmation**
Notes	

Wednesday | 19 June 2024 - Waxing Gibbous

6:00		**Today's quick wins**	
7:00			
8:00			
9:00			
10:00			
11:00		**Health and nutrition**	
12:00			
13:00			
14:00		**Today, I am grateful for...**	
15:00			
16:00			
17:00		**Today's self care**	
18:00			
19:00			
20:00		**Chart your cycle**	
21:00			
22:00			
23:00		**Positive affirmation**	

Notes

Thursday | 20 June 2024 - Waxing Gibbous

6:00	**Today's quick wins**
7:00	
8:00	
9:00	
10:00	
11:00	**Health and nutrition**
12:00	
13:00	
14:00	**Today, I am grateful for...**
15:00	
16:00	
17:00	**Today's self care**
18:00	
19:00	
20:00	**Chart your cycle**
21:00	
22:00	
23:00	**Positive affirmation**

Notes

Friday | 21 June 2024 - Waxing Gibbous

6:00	**Today's quick wins**
7:00	
8:00	
9:00	
10:00	
11:00	**Health and nutrition**
12:00	
13:00	
14:00	**Today, I am grateful for...**
15:00	
16:00	
17:00	**Today's self care**
18:00	
19:00	
20:00	**Chart your cycle**
21:00	
22:00	
23:00	**Positive affirmation**

Notes

Saturday | 22 June 2024 - Full Moon in Capricorn 01.07 GMT

6:00	**Today's quick wins**
7:00	
8:00	
9:00	
10:00	
11:00	**Health and nutrition**
12:00	
13:00	
14:00	**Today, I am grateful for...**
15:00	
16:00	
17:00	**Today's self care**
18:00	
19:00	
20:00	**Chart your cycle**
21:00	
22:00	
23:00	**Positive affirmation**
Notes	

Sunday | 23 June 2024 - Waning Gibbous

6:00		Today's quick wins
7:00		
8:00		
9:00		
10:00		
11:00		Health and nutrition
12:00		
13:00		
14:00		Today, I am grateful for...
15:00		
16:00		
17:00		Today's self care
18:00		
19:00		
20:00		Chart your cycle
21:00		
22:00		
23:00		Positive affirmation
Notes		

Monday | 24 June 2024 - Waning Gibbous

6:00	**Today's quick wins**
7:00	
8:00	
9:00	
10:00	
11:00	**Health and nutrition**
12:00	
13:00	
14:00	**Today, I am grateful for...**
15:00	
16:00	
17:00	**Today's self care**
18:00	
19:00	
20:00	**Chart your cycle**
21:00	
22:00	
23:00	**Positive affirmation**

Notes

Tuesday | 25 June 2024 - Waning Gibbous

6:00	**Today's quick wins**
7:00	
8:00	
9:00	
10:00	
11:00	**Health and nutrition**
12:00	
13:00	
14:00	**Today, I am grateful for…**
15:00	
16:00	
17:00	**Today's self care**
18:00	
19:00	
20:00	**Chart your cycle**
21:00	
22:00	
23:00	**Positive affirmation**

Notes

Wednesday | 26 June 2024 - Waning Gibbous

6:00	**Today's quick wins**
7:00	
8:00	
9:00	
10:00	
11:00	**Health and nutrition**
12:00	
13:00	
14:00	**Today, I am grateful for...**
15:00	
16:00	
17:00	**Today's self care**
18:00	
19:00	
20:00	**Chart your cycle**
21:00	
22:00	
23:00	**Positive affirmation**

Notes

Thursday | 27 June 2024 - Waning Gibbous

6:00	**Today's quick wins**
7:00	
8:00	
9:00	
10:00	
11:00	**Health and nutrition**
12:00	
13:00	
14:00	**Today, I am grateful for...**
15:00	
16:00	
17:00	**Today's self care**
18:00	
19:00	
20:00	**Chart your cycle**
21:00	
22:00	
23:00	**Positive affirmation**

Notes

Friday | 28 June 2024 - Last Quarter

6:00	**Today's quick wins**
7:00	
8:00	
9:00	
10:00	
11:00	**Health and nutrition**
12:00	
13:00	
14:00	**Today, I am grateful for...**
15:00	
16:00	
17:00	**Today's self care**
18:00	
19:00	
20:00	**Chart your cycle**
21:00	
22:00	
23:00	**Positive affirmation**
Notes	

Saturday | 29 June 2024 - Waning Crescent

6:00		Today's quick wins
7:00		
8:00		
9:00		
10:00		
11:00		Health and nutrition
12:00		
13:00		
14:00		Today, I am grateful for...
15:00		
16:00		
17:00		Today's self care
18:00		
19:00		
20:00		Chart your cycle
21:00		
22:00		
23:00		Positive affirmation
Notes		

Sunday | 30 June 2024 - Waning Crescent

6:00	**Today's quick wins**
7:00	
8:00	
9:00	
10:00	
11:00	**Health and nutrition**
12:00	
13:00	
14:00	**Today, I am grateful for...**
15:00	
16:00	
17:00	**Today's self care**
18:00	
19:00	
20:00	**Chart your cycle**
21:00	
22:00	
23:00	**Positive affirmation**

Notes

June achievements

Be proud of yourself and all that you have achieved this month. Write down your wins, big and small. If you have not achieved everything that you set out to do, that's okay! We learn and grow through our mistakes and experiences. You can use this space to make notes about anything that you have learned.

'Live life as if everything is rigged in your favour'
— Rumi

July 2024

Notes	Monday	Tuesday	Wednesday
	1	2	3
	8	9	10
	15	16	17
	22	23	24
	29	30	31

Thursday	Friday	Saturday	Sunday
4	5 ●	6	7
11	12	13 ◐	14
18	19	20	21 ○
25	26	27	28 ◑
1	2	3	4

July
Goddess Sekhmet

SEKHMET

Lioness goddess of war and healing.

She has the power to both protect and destroy. Worshipped as a warrior who looked after doctors and medicine.

She was well known for her rage. We humans have been taught that anger is a 'bad' emotion. But, in reality all emotions are valid, and it is important that we allow ourselves to feel what comes up in our bodies, without bypassing anger. This powerful emotion can be transmuted into something good and helpful when we allow it to move through gently by doing a practices such as tapping or just dancing out the energy. We emerge clearer headed allowing us to come up with solutions to our problems.

Books: Sacred Anger by Seryna Myers
Song: Sekhmet Frequency by Elsa Field, Jerome Zoran and Lorye Hopper
Moon phase: Lunar Eclipse
Crystal: Ruby

My Vision for July

Monday | 1 July 2024 - Waning Crescent

6:00		Today's quick wins
7:00		
8:00		
9:00		
10:00		
11:00		Health and nutrition
12:00		
13:00		
14:00		Today, I am grateful for...
15:00		
16:00		
17:00		Today's self care
18:00		
19:00		
20:00		Chart your cycle
21:00		
22:00		
23:00		Positive affirmation
Notes		

Tuesday | 2 July 2024 - Waning Crescent

6:00	**Today's quick wins**
7:00	
8:00	
9:00	
10:00	
11:00	**Health and nutrition**
12:00	
13:00	
14:00	**Today, I am grateful for...**
15:00	
16:00	
17:00	**Today's self care**
18:00	
19:00	
20:00	**Chart your cycle**
21:00	
22:00	
23:00	**Positive affirmation**
Notes	

Wednesday | 3 July 2024 - Waning Crescent

6:00		**Today's quick wins**	
7:00			
8:00			
9:00			
10:00			
11:00		**Health and nutrition**	
12:00			
13:00			
14:00		**Today, I am grateful for...**	
15:00			
16:00			
17:00		**Today's self care**	
18:00			
19:00			
20:00		**Chart your cycle**	
21:00			
22:00			
23:00		**Positive affirmation**	

Notes

Thursday | 4 July 2024 - Waning Crescent

6:00	**Today's quick wins**
7:00	
8:00	
9:00	
10:00	
11:00	**Health and nutrition**
12:00	
13:00	
14:00	**Today, I am grateful for...**
15:00	
16:00	
17:00	**Today's self care**
18:00	
19:00	
20:00	**Chart your cycle**
21:00	
22:00	
23:00	**Positive affirmation**
Notes	

Friday | 5 July 2024 - New Moon in Cancer 22.57 GMT

6:00		Today's quick wins	
7:00			
8:00			
9:00			
10:00			
11:00		Health and nutrition	
12:00			
13:00			
14:00		Today, I am grateful for...	
15:00			
16:00			
17:00		Today's self care	
18:00			
19:00			
20:00		Chart your cycle	
21:00			
22:00			
23:00		Positive affirmation	

Notes

Saturday | 6 July 2024 - Waxing Crescent

6:00	**Today's quick wins**
7:00	
8:00	
9:00	
10:00	
11:00	**Health and nutrition**
12:00	
13:00	
14:00	**Today, I am grateful for...**
15:00	
16:00	
17:00	**Today's self care**
18:00	
19:00	
20:00	**Chart your cycle**
21:00	
22:00	
23:00	**Positive affirmation**
Notes	

Sunday | 7 July 2024 - Waxing Crescent

6:00	Today's quick wins	
7:00		
8:00		
9:00		
10:00		
11:00	Health and nutrition	
12:00		
13:00		
14:00	Today, I am grateful for...	
15:00		
16:00		
17:00	Today's self care	
18:00		
19:00		
20:00	Chart your cycle	
21:00		
22:00		
23:00	Positive affirmation	
Notes		

Monday | 8 July 2024 - Waxing Crescent

6:00	**Today's quick wins**
7:00	
8:00	
9:00	
10:00	
11:00	**Health and nutrition**
12:00	
13:00	
14:00	**Today, I am grateful for...**
15:00	
16:00	
17:00	**Today's self care**
18:00	
19:00	
20:00	**Chart your cycle**
21:00	
22:00	
23:00	**Positive affirmation**
Notes	

Tuesday | 9 July 2024 - Waxing Crescent

6:00		Today's quick wins
7:00		
8:00		
9:00		
10:00		
11:00		Health and nutrition
12:00		
13:00		
14:00		Today, I am grateful for...
15:00		
16:00		
17:00		Today's self care
18:00		
19:00		
20:00		Chart your cycle
21:00		
22:00		
23:00		Positive affirmation

Notes

Wednesday | 10 July 2024 - Waxing Crescent

6:00		**Today's quick wins**	
7:00			
8:00			
9:00			
10:00			
11:00		**Health and nutrition**	
12:00			
13:00			
14:00		**Today, I am grateful for...**	
15:00			
16:00			
17:00		**Today's self care**	
18:00			
19:00			
20:00		**Chart your cycle**	
21:00			
22:00			
23:00		**Positive affirmation**	

Notes

Thursday | 11 July 2024 - Waxing Crescent

6:00	Today's quick wins	
7:00		
8:00		
9:00		
10:00		
11:00	Health and nutrition	
12:00		
13:00		
14:00	Today, I am grateful for...	
15:00		
16:00		
17:00	Today's self care	
18:00		
19:00		
20:00	Chart your cycle	
21:00		
22:00		
23:00	Positive affirmation	
Notes		

Friday | 12 July 2024 - Waxing Crescent

6:00	**Today's quick wins**
7:00	
8:00	
9:00	
10:00	
11:00	**Health and nutrition**
12:00	
13:00	
14:00	**Today, I am grateful for...**
15:00	
16:00	
17:00	**Today's self care**
18:00	
19:00	
20:00	**Chart your cycle**
21:00	
22:00	
23:00	**Positive affirmation**
Notes	

Saturday | 13 July 2024 - First Quarter

6:00	**Today's quick wins**
7:00	
8:00	
9:00	
10:00	
11:00	**Health and nutrition**
12:00	
13:00	
14:00	**Today, I am grateful for...**
15:00	
16:00	
17:00	**Today's self care**
18:00	
19:00	
20:00	**Chart your cycle**
21:00	
22:00	
23:00	**Positive affirmation**

Notes

Sunday | 14 July 2024 - First Quarter

6:00	Today's quick wins
7:00	
8:00	
9:00	
10:00	
11:00	Health and nutrition
12:00	
13:00	
14:00	Today, I am grateful for...
15:00	
16:00	
17:00	Today's self care
18:00	
19:00	
20:00	Chart your cycle
21:00	
22:00	
23:00	Positive affirmation

Notes

Monday | 15 July 2024 - Waxing Gibbous

6:00		**Today's quick wins**	
7:00			
8:00			
9:00			
10:00			
11:00		**Health and nutrition**	
12:00			
13:00			
14:00		**Today, I am grateful for...**	
15:00			
16:00			
17:00		**Today's self care**	
18:00			
19:00			
20:00		**Chart your cycle**	
21:00			
22:00			
23:00		**Positive affirmation**	

Notes

Tuesday | 16 July 2024 - Waxing Gibbous

6:00	**Today's quick wins**
7:00	
8:00	
9:00	
10:00	
11:00	**Health and nutrition**
12:00	
13:00	
14:00	**Today, I am grateful for...**
15:00	
16:00	
17:00	**Today's self care**
18:00	
19:00	
20:00	**Chart your cycle**
21:00	
22:00	
23:00	**Positive affirmation**
Notes	

Wednesday | 17 July 2024 - Waxing Gibbous

6:00		**Today's quick wins**	
7:00			
8:00			
9:00			
10:00			
11:00		**Health and nutrition**	
12:00			
13:00			
14:00		**Today, I am grateful for...**	
15:00			
16:00			
17:00		**Today's self care**	
18:00			
19:00			
20:00		**Chart your cycle**	
21:00			
22:00			
23:00		**Positive affirmation**	
Notes			

Thursday | 18 July 2024 - Waxing Gibbous

6:00	**Today's quick wins**
7:00	
8:00	
9:00	
10:00	
11:00	**Health and nutrition**
12:00	
13:00	
14:00	**Today, I am grateful for...**
15:00	
16:00	
17:00	**Today's self care**
18:00	
19:00	
20:00	**Chart your cycle**
21:00	
22:00	
23:00	**Positive affirmation**

Notes

Friday | 19 July 2024 - Waxing Gibbous

6:00		**Today's quick wins**	
7:00			
8:00			
9:00			
10:00			
11:00		**Health and nutrition**	
12:00			
13:00			
14:00		**Today, I am grateful for...**	
15:00			
16:00			
17:00		**Today's self care**	
18:00			
19:00			
20:00		**Chart your cycle**	
21:00			
22:00			
23:00		**Positive affirmation**	
Notes			

Saturday | 20 July 2024 - Waxing Gibbous

6:00	**Today's quick wins**
7:00	
8:00	
9:00	
10:00	
11:00	**Health and nutrition**
12:00	
13:00	
14:00	**Today, I am grateful for…**
15:00	
16:00	
17:00	**Today's self care**
18:00	
19:00	
20:00	**Chart your cycle**
21:00	
22:00	
23:00	**Positive affirmation**
Notes	

Sunday | 21 July 2024 - Full Moon in Capricorn 10.16 GMT

6:00	Today's quick wins	
7:00		
8:00		
9:00		
10:00		
11:00	Health and nutrition	
12:00		
13:00		
14:00	Today, I am grateful for...	
15:00		
16:00		
17:00	Today's self care	
18:00		
19:00		
20:00	Chart your cycle	
21:00		
22:00		
23:00	Positive affirmation	
Notes		

Monday | 22 July 2024 - Waning Gibbous

6:00	Today's quick wins	
7:00		
8:00		
9:00		
10:00		
11:00	Health and nutrition	
12:00		
13:00		
14:00	Today, I am grateful for...	
15:00		
16:00		
17:00	Today's self care	
18:00		
19:00		
20:00	Chart your cycle	
21:00		
22:00		
23:00	Positive affirmation	
Notes		

Tuesday | 23 July 2024 - Waning Gibbous

6:00		**Today's quick wins**
7:00		
8:00		
9:00		
10:00		
11:00		**Health and nutrition**
12:00		
13:00		
14:00		**Today, I am grateful for...**
15:00		
16:00		
17:00		**Today's self care**
18:00		
19:00		
20:00		**Chart your cycle**
21:00		
22:00		
23:00		**Positive affirmation**

Notes

Wednesday | 24 July 2024 - Waning Gibbous

6:00	**Today's quick wins**
7:00	
8:00	
9:00	
10:00	
11:00	**Health and nutrition**
12:00	
13:00	
14:00	**Today, I am grateful for...**
15:00	
16:00	
17:00	**Today's self care**
18:00	
19:00	
20:00	**Chart your cycle**
21:00	
22:00	
23:00	**Positive affirmation**
Notes	

Thursday | 25 July 2024 - Waning Gibbous

6:00		Today's quick wins
7:00		
8:00		
9:00		
10:00		
11:00		Health and nutrition
12:00		
13:00		
14:00		Today, I am grateful for...
15:00		
16:00		
17:00		Today's self care
18:00		
19:00		
20:00		Chart your cycle
21:00		
22:00		
23:00		Positive affirmation
Notes		

Friday | 26 July 2024 - Waning Gibbous

6:00	**Today's quick wins**
7:00	
8:00	
9:00	
10:00	
11:00	**Health and nutrition**
12:00	
13:00	
14:00	**Today, I am grateful for...**
15:00	
16:00	
17:00	**Today's self care**
18:00	
19:00	
20:00	**Chart your cycle**
21:00	
22:00	
23:00	**Positive affirmation**

Notes

Saturday | 27 July 2024 - Waning Gibbous

6:00		**Today's quick wins**	
7:00			
8:00			
9:00			
10:00			
11:00		**Health and nutrition**	
12:00			
13:00			
14:00		**Today, I am grateful for...**	
15:00			
16:00			
17:00		**Today's self care**	
18:00			
19:00			
20:00		**Chart your cycle**	
21:00			
22:00			
23:00		**Positive affirmation**	

Notes

Sunday | 28 July 2024 - Last Quarter

6:00		Today's quick wins
7:00		
8:00		
9:00		
10:00		
11:00		Health and nutrition
12:00		
13:00		
14:00		Today, I am grateful for...
15:00		
16:00		
17:00		Today's self care
18:00		
19:00		
20:00		Chart your cycle
21:00		
22:00		
23:00		Positive affirmation
Notes		

Monday | 29 July 2024 - Waning Crescent

6:00		**Today's quick wins**	
7:00			
8:00			
9:00			
10:00			
11:00		**Health and nutrition**	
12:00			
13:00			
14:00		**Today, I am grateful for…**	
15:00			
16:00			
17:00		**Today's self care**	
18:00			
19:00			
20:00		**Chart your cycle**	
21:00			
22:00			
23:00		**Positive affirmation**	

Notes

Tuesday | 30 July 2024 - Waning Crescent

6:00	**Today's quick wins**
7:00	
8:00	
9:00	
10:00	
11:00	**Health and nutrition**
12:00	
13:00	
14:00	**Today, I am grateful for...**
15:00	
16:00	
17:00	**Today's self care**
18:00	
19:00	
20:00	**Chart your cycle**
21:00	
22:00	
23:00	**Positive affirmation**

Notes

Wednesday | 31 July 2024 - Waning Crescent

6:00		**Today's quick wins**	
7:00			
8:00			
9:00			
10:00			
11:00		**Health and nutrition**	
12:00			
13:00			
14:00		**Today, I am grateful for…**	
15:00			
16:00			
17:00		**Today's self care**	
18:00			
19:00			
20:00		**Chart your cycle**	
21:00			
22:00			
23:00		**Positive affirmation**	

Notes

July achievements

Be proud of yourself and all that you have achieved this month. Write down your wins, big and small. If you have not achieved everything that you set out to do, that's okay! We learn and grow through our mistakes and experiences. You can use this space to make notes about anything that you have learned.

August 2024

Notes	Monday	Tuesday	Wednesday
	5	6	7
	12	13	14
	19	20	21
	26	27	28

Thursday	Friday	Saturday	Sunday
1	2	3	4 ●
8	9	10	11
15	16	17	18
22	23	24	25
29	30	31	1

August
Goddess Diana

DIANA

Roman goddess of the moon, hunting and wild animals.

She is a wild spirit, advenutre seeker and guardian of the countryside.

The ancient Romans celebrated her during Nemoralia, the festival of torches, on the 13th of August. Women would take ceremonial baths, put flowers in their hair and carry candles to lakes and rivers to thank Diana for granting their wishes. Requests were written on ribbons and tied to altars. The killing of animals was forbidden on this day.

We connect to her when we are wild swimming, hiking and generally running free in the great outdoors.

Books: The Quiet Moon: Pathways to an Ancient Way of Being by Kevin Parr
Song: Into the wild by Shylah Ray Sunshine
Moon phase: Crescent moon
Crystal: Amethyst

My Vision for August

Thursday | 1 August 2024 - Waning Crescent

6:00	Today's quick wins	
7:00		
8:00		
9:00		
10:00		
11:00	Health and nutrition	
12:00		
13:00		
14:00	Today, I am grateful for...	
15:00		
16:00		
17:00	Today's self care	
18:00		
19:00		
20:00	Chart your cycle	
21:00		
22:00		
23:00	Positive affirmation	

Notes

Friday | 2 August 2024 - Waning Crescent

6:00	**Today's quick wins**
7:00	
8:00	
9:00	
10:00	
11:00	**Health and nutrition**
12:00	
13:00	
14:00	**Today, I am grateful for...**
15:00	
16:00	
17:00	**Today's self care**
18:00	
19:00	
20:00	**Chart your cycle**
21:00	
22:00	
23:00	**Positive affirmation**

Notes

Saturday | 3 August 2024 - Waning Crescent

6:00		Today's quick wins	
7:00			
8:00			
9:00			
10:00			
11:00		Health and nutrition	
12:00			
13:00			
14:00		Today, I am grateful for...	
15:00			
16:00			
17:00		Today's self care	
18:00			
19:00			
20:00		Chart your cycle	
21:00			
22:00			
23:00		Positive affirmation	

Notes

Sunday | 4 August 2024 - New Moon in Leo 11.12 GMT

6:00	**Today's quick wins**
7:00	
8:00	
9:00	
10:00	
11:00	**Health and nutrition**
12:00	
13:00	
14:00	**Today, I am grateful for...**
15:00	
16:00	
17:00	**Today's self care**
18:00	
19:00	
20:00	**Chart your cycle**
21:00	
22:00	
23:00	**Positive affirmation**
Notes	

Monday | 5 August 2024 - Waxing Crescent

6:00		Today's quick wins
7:00		
8:00		
9:00		
10:00		
11:00		Health and nutrition
12:00		
13:00		
14:00		Today, I am grateful for...
15:00		
16:00		
17:00		Today's self care
18:00		
19:00		
20:00		Chart your cycle
21:00		
22:00		
23:00		Positive affirmation

Notes

Tuesday | 6 August 2024 - Waxing Crescent

6:00	**Today's quick wins**
7:00	
8:00	
9:00	
10:00	
11:00	**Health and nutrition**
12:00	
13:00	
14:00	**Today, I am grateful for...**
15:00	
16:00	
17:00	**Today's self care**
18:00	
19:00	
20:00	**Chart your cycle**
21:00	
22:00	
23:00	**Positive affirmation**
Notes	

Wednesday | 7 August 2024 - Waxing Crescent

6:00		**Today's quick wins**	
7:00			
8:00			
9:00			
10:00			
11:00		**Health and nutrition**	
12:00			
13:00			
14:00		**Today, I am grateful for...**	
15:00			
16:00			
17:00		**Today's self care**	
18:00			
19:00			
20:00		**Chart your cycle**	
21:00			
22:00			
23:00		**Positive affirmation**	

Notes

Thursday | 8 August 2024 - Waxing Crescent

6:00		**Today's quick wins**	
7:00			
8:00			
9:00			
10:00			
11:00		**Health and nutrition**	
12:00			
13:00			
14:00		**Today, I am grateful for...**	
15:00			
16:00			
17:00		**Today's self care**	
18:00			
19:00			
20:00		**Chart your cycle**	
21:00			
22:00			
23:00		**Positive affirmation**	

Notes

Friday | 9 August 2024 - Waxing Crescent

6:00		Today's quick wins	
7:00			
8:00			
9:00			
10:00			
11:00		Health and nutrition	
12:00			
13:00			
14:00		Today, I am grateful for...	
15:00			
16:00			
17:00		Today's self care	
18:00			
19:00			
20:00		Chart your cycle	
21:00			
22:00			
23:00		Positive affirmation	

Notes

Saturday | 10 August 2024 - Waxing Crescent

6:00	**Today's quick wins**
7:00	
8:00	
9:00	
10:00	
11:00	**Health and nutrition**
12:00	
13:00	
14:00	**Today, I am grateful for...**
15:00	
16:00	
17:00	**Today's self care**
18:00	
19:00	
20:00	**Chart your cycle**
21:00	
22:00	
23:00	**Positive affirmation**

Notes

Sunday | 11 August 2024 - Waxing Crescent

6:00	**Today's quick wins**
7:00	
8:00	
9:00	
10:00	
11:00	**Health and nutrition**
12:00	
13:00	
14:00	**Today, I am grateful for...**
15:00	
16:00	
17:00	**Today's self care**
18:00	
19:00	
20:00	**Chart your cycle**
21:00	
22:00	
23:00	**Positive affirmation**

Notes

Monday | 12 August 2024 - First Quarter

6:00	Today's quick wins
7:00	
8:00	
9:00	
10:00	
11:00	Health and nutrition
12:00	
13:00	
14:00	Today, I am grateful for...
15:00	
16:00	
17:00	Today's self care
18:00	
19:00	
20:00	Chart your cycle
21:00	
22:00	
23:00	Positive affirmation
Notes	

Tuesday | 13 August 2024 - Waxing Gibbous

6:00	**Today's quick wins**
7:00	
8:00	
9:00	
10:00	
11:00	**Health and nutrition**
12:00	
13:00	
14:00	**Today, I am grateful for...**
15:00	
16:00	
17:00	**Today's self care**
18:00	
19:00	
20:00	**Chart your cycle**
21:00	
22:00	
23:00	**Positive affirmation**
Notes	

Wednesday | 14 August 2024 - Waxing Gibbous

6:00	Today's quick wins	
7:00		
8:00		
9:00		
10:00		
11:00	Health and nutrition	
12:00		
13:00		
14:00	Today, I am grateful for...	
15:00		
16:00		
17:00	Today's self care	
18:00		
19:00		
20:00	Chart your cycle	
21:00		
22:00		
23:00	Positive affirmation	

Notes

Thursday | 15 August 2024 - Waxing Gibbous

6:00		**Today's quick wins**	
7:00			
8:00			
9:00			
10:00			
11:00		**Health and nutrition**	
12:00			
13:00			
14:00		**Today, I am grateful for…**	
15:00			
16:00			
17:00		**Today's self care**	
18:00			
19:00			
20:00		**Chart your cycle**	
21:00			
22:00			
23:00		**Positive affirmation**	
Notes			

Friday | 16 August 2024 - Waxing Gibbous

6:00	**Today's quick wins**
7:00	
8:00	
9:00	
10:00	
11:00	**Health and nutrition**
12:00	
13:00	
14:00	**Today, I am grateful for...**
15:00	
16:00	
17:00	**Today's self care**
18:00	
19:00	
20:00	**Chart your cycle**
21:00	
22:00	
23:00	**Positive affirmation**
Notes	

Saturday | 17 August 2024 - Waxing Gibbous

6:00		**Today's quick wins**	
7:00			
8:00			
9:00			
10:00			
11:00		**Health and nutrition**	
12:00			
13:00			
14:00		**Today, I am grateful for...**	
15:00			
16:00			
17:00		**Today's self care**	
18:00			
19:00			
20:00		**Chart your cycle**	
21:00			
22:00			
23:00		**Positive affirmation**	

Notes

Sunday | 18 August 2024 - Waxing Gibbous

6:00	**Today's quick wins**
7:00	
8:00	
9:00	
10:00	
11:00	**Health and nutrition**
12:00	
13:00	
14:00	**Today, I am grateful for...**
15:00	
16:00	
17:00	**Today's self care**
18:00	
19:00	
20:00	**Chart your cycle**
21:00	
22:00	
23:00	**Positive affirmation**
Notes	

Monday | 19 August 2024 - Full Moon in Aquarius 18.25 GMT

6:00		Today's quick wins
7:00		
8:00		
9:00		
10:00		
11:00		Health and nutrition
12:00		
13:00		
14:00		Today, I am grateful for…
15:00		
16:00		
17:00		Today's self care
18:00		
19:00		
20:00		Chart your cycle
21:00		
22:00		
23:00		Positive affirmation
Notes		

Tuesday | 20 August 2024 - Waning Gibbous

6:00	**Today's quick wins**
7:00	
8:00	
9:00	
10:00	
11:00	**Health and nutrition**
12:00	
13:00	
14:00	**Today, I am grateful for...**
15:00	
16:00	
17:00	**Today's self care**
18:00	
19:00	
20:00	**Chart your cycle**
21:00	
22:00	
23:00	**Positive affirmation**

Notes

Wednesday | 21 August 2024 - Waning Gibbous

6:00		Today's quick wins	
7:00			
8:00			
9:00			
10:00			
11:00		Health and nutrition	
12:00			
13:00			
14:00		Today, I am grateful for…	
15:00			
16:00			
17:00		Today's self care	
18:00			
19:00			
20:00		Chart your cycle	
21:00			
22:00			
23:00		Positive affirmation	
Notes			

Thursday | 22 August 2024 - Waning Gibbous

6:00		**Today's quick wins**	
7:00			
8:00			
9:00			
10:00			
11:00		**Health and nutrition**	
12:00			
13:00			
14:00		**Today, I am grateful for…**	
15:00			
16:00			
17:00		**Today's self care**	
18:00			
19:00			
20:00		**Chart your cycle**	
21:00			
22:00			
23:00		**Positive affirmation**	

Notes

Friday | 23 August 2024 - Waning Gibbous

6:00		Today's quick wins	
7:00			
8:00			
9:00			
10:00			
11:00		Health and nutrition	
12:00			
13:00			
14:00		Today, I am grateful for…	
15:00			
16:00			
17:00		Today's self care	
18:00			
19:00			
20:00		Chart your cycle	
21:00			
22:00			
23:00		Positive affirmation	

Notes

Saturday | 24 August 2024 - Waning Gibbous

6:00	**Today's quick wins**
7:00	
8:00	
9:00	
10:00	
11:00	**Health and nutrition**
12:00	
13:00	
14:00	**Today, I am grateful for...**
15:00	
16:00	
17:00	**Today's self care**
18:00	
19:00	
20:00	**Chart your cycle**
21:00	
22:00	
23:00	**Positive affirmation**

Notes

Sunday | 25 August 2024 - Waning Gibbous

6:00		Today's quick wins	
7:00			
8:00			
9:00			
10:00			
11:00		Health and nutrition	
12:00			
13:00			
14:00		Today, I am grateful for...	
15:00			
16:00			
17:00		Today's self care	
18:00			
19:00			
20:00		Chart your cycle	
21:00			
22:00			
23:00		Positive affirmation	
Notes			

Monday | 26 August 2024 - Last Quarter

6:00		Today's quick wins
7:00		
8:00		
9:00		
10:00		
11:00		Health and nutrition
12:00		
13:00		
14:00		Today, I am grateful for...
15:00		
16:00		
17:00		Today's self care
18:00		
19:00		
20:00		Chart your cycle
21:00		
22:00		
23:00		Positive affirmation
Notes		

Tuesday | 27 August 2024 - Waning Crescent

6:00		**Today's quick wins**	
7:00			
8:00			
9:00			
10:00			
11:00		**Health and nutrition**	
12:00			
13:00			
14:00		**Today, I am grateful for...**	
15:00			
16:00			
17:00		**Today's self care**	
18:00			
19:00			
20:00		**Chart your cycle**	
21:00			
22:00			
23:00		**Positive affirmation**	

Notes

Wednesday | 28 August 2024 - Waning Crescent

6:00		Today's quick wins
7:00		
8:00		
9:00		
10:00		
11:00		Health and nutrition
12:00		
13:00		
14:00		Today, I am grateful for...
15:00		
16:00		
17:00		Today's self care
18:00		
19:00		
20:00		Chart your cycle
21:00		
22:00		
23:00		Positive affirmation
Notes		

Thursday | 29 August 2024 - Waning Crescent

6:00		Today's quick wins
7:00		
8:00		
9:00		
10:00		
11:00		Health and nutrition
12:00		
13:00		
14:00		Today, I am grateful for...
15:00		
16:00		
17:00		Today's self care
18:00		
19:00		
20:00		Chart your cycle
21:00		
22:00		
23:00		Positive affirmation
Notes		

Friday | 30 August 2024 - Waning Crescent

6:00	**Today's quick wins**
7:00	
8:00	
9:00	
10:00	
11:00	**Health and nutrition**
12:00	
13:00	
14:00	**Today, I am grateful for...**
15:00	
16:00	
17:00	**Today's self care**
18:00	
19:00	
20:00	**Chart your cycle**
21:00	
22:00	
23:00	**Positive affirmation**
Notes	

Saturday | 31 August 2024 - Waning Crescent

6:00	Today's quick wins	
7:00		
8:00		
9:00		
10:00		
11:00	Health and nutrition	
12:00		
13:00		
14:00	Today, I am grateful for...	
15:00		
16:00		
17:00	Today's self care	
18:00		
19:00		
20:00	Chart your cycle	
21:00		
22:00		
23:00	Positive affirmation	
Notes		

August achievements

Be proud of yourself and all that you have achieved this month. Write down your wins, big and small. If you have not achieved everything that you set out to do, that's okay! We learn and grow through our mistakes and experiences. You can use this space to make notes about anything that you have learned.

September 2024

Notes	Sunday	Monday	Tuesday
	1	2	3 ●
	8	9	10
	15	16	17
	22 *Autumn Equinox*	23	24 ☽
	29	30	

Wednesday	Thursday	Friday	Saturday
4	5	6	7
11	12	13	14
18	19	20	21
25	26	27	28
2	3	4	5

September
Goddess Lilith

LILITH

Independence, free will and free speech.

Lilith has been given a bad rap. She was Adams first wife, she left him, craving independence and to be treated as an equal. Adam refused to let her go, but she went anyway and she was punished.

She has been painted as a demon in stories ever since. History tells things one way, but in her-story she chased freedom at any cost and was a feminist icon for living her truth and not playing small.

We were always taught to fear the witches instead of those who burned them alive, the same is true with Lilith. She will forever be known as a demon to those who don't question.....

Book: Embracing Lilith by Mark H.Williams
Song: Lilith by Plaid and Bjork
Crystal: Black Tourmaline
Moon phase: Full Moon

My Vision for September

Sunday | 1 September 2024 - Waning Crescent

6:00	Today's quick wins	
7:00		
8:00		
9:00		
10:00		
11:00	Health and nutrition	
12:00		
13:00		
14:00	Today, I am grateful for...	
15:00		
16:00		
17:00	Today's self care	
18:00		
19:00		
20:00	Chart your cycle	
21:00		
22:00		
23:00	Positive affirmation	
Notes		

Monday | 2 September 2024 - Waning Crescent

Time		Section	
6:00		**Today's quick wins**	
7:00			
8:00			
9:00			
10:00			
11:00		**Health and nutrition**	
12:00			
13:00			
14:00		**Today, I am grateful for...**	
15:00			
16:00			
17:00		**Today's self care**	
18:00			
19:00			
20:00		**Chart your cycle**	
21:00			
22:00			
23:00		**Positive affirmation**	

Notes

Tuesday | 3 September 2024 - New Moon in Virgo 01:55 GMT

6:00		Today's quick wins
7:00		
8:00		
9:00		
10:00		
11:00		Health and nutrition
12:00		
13:00		
14:00		Today, I am grateful for...
15:00		
16:00		
17:00		Today's self care
18:00		
19:00		
20:00		Chart your cycle
21:00		
22:00		
23:00		Positive affirmation
Notes		

Wednesday | 4 September 2024 - Waxing Crescent

Time		Section	
6:00		**Today's quick wins**	
7:00			
8:00			
9:00			
10:00			
11:00		**Health and nutrition**	
12:00			
13:00			
14:00		**Today, I am grateful for...**	
15:00			
16:00			
17:00		**Today's self care**	
18:00			
19:00			
20:00		**Chart your cycle**	
21:00			
22:00			
23:00		**Positive affirmation**	
Notes			

Thursday | 5 September 2024 - Waxing Crescent

Time		Section
6:00		Today's quick wins
7:00		
8:00		
9:00		
10:00		
11:00		Health and nutrition
12:00		
13:00		
14:00		Today, I am grateful for...
15:00		
16:00		
17:00		Today's self care
18:00		
19:00		
20:00		Chart your cycle
21:00		
22:00		
23:00		Positive affirmation
Notes		

Friday | 6 September 2024 - Waxing Crescent

6:00	**Today's quick wins**
7:00	
8:00	
9:00	
10:00	
11:00	**Health and nutrition**
12:00	
13:00	
14:00	**Today, I am grateful for...**
15:00	
16:00	
17:00	**Today's self care**
18:00	
19:00	
20:00	**Chart your cycle**
21:00	
22:00	
23:00	**Positive affirmation**
Notes	

Saturday | 7 September 2024 - Waxing Crescent

6:00	**Today's quick wins**
7:00	
8:00	
9:00	
10:00	
11:00	**Health and nutrition**
12:00	
13:00	
14:00	**Today, I am grateful for...**
15:00	
16:00	
17:00	**Today's self care**
18:00	
19:00	
20:00	**Chart your cycle**
21:00	
22:00	
23:00	**Positive affirmation**

Notes

Sunday | 8 September 2024 - Waxing Crescent

Time		Section	
6:00		Today's quick wins	
7:00			
8:00			
9:00			
10:00			
11:00		Health and nutrition	
12:00			
13:00			
14:00		Today, I am grateful for...	
15:00			
16:00			
17:00		Today's self care	
18:00			
19:00			
20:00		Chart your cycle	
21:00			
22:00			
23:00		Positive affirmation	
Notes			

Monday | 9 September 2024 - Waxing Crescent

6:00		Today's quick wins	
7:00			
8:00			
9:00			
10:00			
11:00		Health and nutrition	
12:00			
13:00			
14:00		Today, I am grateful for...	
15:00			
16:00			
17:00		Today's self care	
18:00			
19:00			
20:00		Chart your cycle	
21:00			
22:00			
23:00		Positive affirmation	

Notes

Tuesday | 10 September - Waxing Crescent

6:00	**Today's quick wins**
7:00	
8:00	
9:00	
10:00	
11:00	**Health and nutrition**
12:00	
13:00	
14:00	**Today, I am grateful for…**
15:00	
16:00	
17:00	**Today's self care**
18:00	
19:00	
20:00	**Chart your cycle**
21:00	
22:00	
23:00	**Positive affirmation**

Notes

Wednesday | 11 September 2024 - First Quarter

6:00		Today's quick wins
7:00		
8:00		
9:00		
10:00		
11:00		Health and nutrition
12:00		
13:00		
14:00		Today, I am grateful for…
15:00		
16:00		
17:00		Today's self care
18:00		
19:00		
20:00		Chart your cycle
21:00		
22:00		
23:00		Positive affirmation

Notes

Thursday | 12 September 2024 - Waxing Gibbous

6:00	**Today's quick wins**
7:00	
8:00	
9:00	
10:00	
11:00	**Health and nutrition**
12:00	
13:00	
14:00	**Today, I am grateful for...**
15:00	
16:00	
17:00	**Today's self care**
18:00	
19:00	
20:00	**Chart your cycle**
21:00	
22:00	
23:00	**Positive affirmation**

Notes

Friday | 13 September 2024 - Waxing Gibbous

6:00		Today's quick wins
7:00		
8:00		
9:00		
10:00		
11:00		Health and nutrition
12:00		
13:00		
14:00		Today, I am grateful for...
15:00		
16:00		
17:00		Today's self care
18:00		
19:00		
20:00		Chart your cycle
21:00		
22:00		
23:00		Positive affirmation
Notes		

Saturday | 14 September 2024 - Waxing Gibbous

6:00	**Today's quick wins**
7:00	
8:00	
9:00	
10:00	
11:00	**Health and nutrition**
12:00	
13:00	
14:00	**Today, I am grateful for...**
15:00	
16:00	
17:00	**Today's self care**
18:00	
19:00	
20:00	**Chart your cycle**
21:00	
22:00	
23:00	**Positive affirmation**
Notes	

Sunday | 15 September 2024 - Waxing Gibbous

6:00		Today's quick wins
7:00		
8:00		
9:00		
10:00		
11:00		Health and nutrition
12:00		
13:00		
14:00		Today, I am grateful for…
15:00		
16:00		
17:00		Today's self care
18:00		
19:00		
20:00		Chart your cycle
21:00		
22:00		
23:00		Positive affirmation

Notes

Monday | 16 September 2024 - Waxing Gibbous

6:00		Today's quick wins
7:00		
8:00		
9:00		
10:00		
11:00		Health and nutrition
12:00		
13:00		
14:00		Today, I am grateful for...
15:00		
16:00		
17:00		Today's self care
18:00		
19:00		
20:00		Chart your cycle
21:00		
22:00		
23:00		Positive affirmation
Notes		

Tuesday | 17 September 2024 - Waxing Gibbous

6:00	Today's quick wins	
7:00		
8:00		
9:00		
10:00		
11:00	Health and nutrition	
12:00		
13:00		
14:00	Today, I am grateful for...	
15:00		
16:00		
17:00	Today's self care	
18:00		
19:00		
20:00	Chart your cycle	
21:00		
22:00		
23:00	Positive affirmation	
Notes		

Wednesday | 18 September 2024

Full Moon Lunar Eclipse in Pisces 02.34 GMT

6:00	**Today's quick wins**
7:00	
8:00	
9:00	
10:00	
11:00	**Health and nutrition**
12:00	
13:00	
14:00	**Today, I am grateful for...**
15:00	
16:00	
17:00	**Today's self care**
18:00	
19:00	
20:00	**Chart your cycle**
21:00	
22:00	
23:00	**Positive affirmation**

Notes

Thursday | 19 September 2024 - Waning Gibbous

6:00		**Today's quick wins**
7:00		
8:00		
9:00		
10:00		
11:00		**Health and nutrition**
12:00		
13:00		
14:00		**Today, I am grateful for...**
15:00		
16:00		
17:00		**Today's self care**
18:00		
19:00		
20:00		**Chart your cycle**
21:00		
22:00		
23:00		**Positive affirmation**
Notes		

Friday | 20 September 2024 - Waning Gibbous

6:00		Today's quick wins
7:00		
8:00		
9:00		
10:00		
11:00		Health and nutrition
12:00		
13:00		
14:00		Today, I am grateful for...
15:00		
16:00		
17:00		Today's self care
18:00		
19:00		
20:00		Chart your cycle
21:00		
22:00		
23:00		Positive affirmation
Notes		

Saturday | 21 September 2024 - Waning Gibbous

6:00		Today's quick wins	
7:00			
8:00			
9:00			
10:00			
11:00		Health and nutrition	
12:00			
13:00			
14:00		Today, I am grateful for...	
15:00			
16:00			
17:00		Today's self care	
18:00			
19:00			
20:00		Chart your cycle	
21:00			
22:00			
23:00		Positive affirmation	

Notes

Sunday | 22 September 2024 - Waning Gibbous

6:00	Today's quick wins
7:00	
8:00	
9:00	
10:00	
11:00	Health and nutrition
12:00	
13:00	
14:00	Today, I am grateful for...
15:00	
16:00	
17:00	Today's self care
18:00	
19:00	
20:00	Chart your cycle
21:00	
22:00	
23:00	Positive affirmation
Notes	

Monday | 23 September 2024 - Waning Gibbous

6:00	Today's quick wins	
7:00		
8:00		
9:00		
10:00		
11:00	Health and nutrition	
12:00		
13:00		
14:00	Today, I am grateful for…	
15:00		
16:00		
17:00	Today's self care	
18:00		
19:00		
20:00	Chart your cycle	
21:00		
22:00		
23:00	Positive affirmation	

Notes

Tuesday | 24 September 2024 - Last Quarter

6:00	**Today's quick wins**
7:00	
8:00	
9:00	
10:00	
11:00	**Health and nutrition**
12:00	
13:00	
14:00	**Today, I am grateful for...**
15:00	
16:00	
17:00	**Today's self care**
18:00	
19:00	
20:00	**Chart your cycle**
21:00	
22:00	
23:00	**Positive affirmation**

Notes

Wednesday | 25 September - Waning Crescent

6:00		Today's quick wins	
7:00			
8:00			
9:00			
10:00			
11:00		Health and nutrition	
12:00			
13:00			
14:00		Today, I am grateful for...	
15:00			
16:00			
17:00		Today's self care	
18:00			
19:00			
20:00		Chart your cycle	
21:00			
22:00			
23:00		Positive affirmation	
Notes			

Thursday | 26 September 2024 - Waning Crescent

6:00	**Today's quick wins**
7:00	
8:00	
9:00	
10:00	
11:00	**Health and nutrition**
12:00	
13:00	
14:00	**Today, I am grateful for...**
15:00	
16:00	
17:00	**Today's self care**
18:00	
19:00	
20:00	**Chart your cycle**
21:00	
22:00	
23:00	**Positive affirmation**
Notes	

Friday | 27 September 2024 - Waning Crescent

6:00		Today's quick wins
7:00		
8:00		
9:00		
10:00		
11:00		Health and nutrition
12:00		
13:00		
14:00		Today, I am grateful for…
15:00		
16:00		
17:00		Today's self care
18:00		
19:00		
20:00		Chart your cycle
21:00		
22:00		
23:00		Positive affirmation

Notes

Saturday | 28 September 2024 - Waning Crescent

6:00	**Today's quick wins**
7:00	
8:00	
9:00	
10:00	
11:00	**Health and nutrition**
12:00	
13:00	
14:00	**Today, I am grateful for...**
15:00	
16:00	
17:00	**Today's self care**
18:00	
19:00	
20:00	**Chart your cycle**
21:00	
22:00	
23:00	**Positive affirmation**
Notes	

Sunday | 29 September 2024 - Waning Crescent

6:00	Today's quick wins	
7:00		
8:00		
9:00		
10:00		
11:00	Health and nutrition	
12:00		
13:00		
14:00	Today, I am grateful for…	
15:00		
16:00		
17:00	Today's self care	
18:00		
19:00		
20:00	Chart your cycle	
21:00		
22:00		
23:00	Positive affirmation	
Notes		

Monday | 30 September 2024 - Waning Crescent

6:00	**Today's quick wins**
7:00	
8:00	
9:00	
10:00	
11:00	**Health and nutrition**
12:00	
13:00	
14:00	**Today, I am grateful for...**
15:00	
16:00	
17:00	**Today's self care**
18:00	
19:00	
20:00	**Chart your cycle**
21:00	
22:00	
23:00	**Positive affirmation**
Notes	

September achievements

Be proud of yourself and all that you have achieved this month. Write down your wins, big and small. If you have not achieved everything that you set out to do, that's okay! We learn and grow through our mistakes and experiences. You can use this space to make notes about anything that you have learned.

"You are a function of what the whole universe is doing in the same way that a wave is a function of what the whole ocean is doing."

– Alan Watts

October 2024

Notes	Monday	Tuesday	Wednesday
		1	2
	7	8	9
	14	15	16
	21	22	23
	28	29	30

Thursday	Friday	Saturday	Sunday
3	4	5	6
10 ◐	11	12	13
17 ○	18	19	20
24 ◑	25	26	27
31	1	2	3

October
Goddess Hecate

HECATE

Goddess of witchcraft and magic.

She was adopted into the Greek pantheon, but Hecate can be traced much further back than ancient Greece. The Greeks used to put shrines to her at road intersections. She is said to be a guide we can look to when we dont know which path to choose in life.

Sometimes depicted as a triple headed goddess, she is associated with the underworld, heaven and Earth (birth, life and death). She can see things from many angles. Hecate has a powerful energy and is happy to shine a light for those who are lost.

The original witch, knows her boundaries and is not to be messed with.

Books: Witches, Nurses and Midwives by Barbara Ehrenreich and Deirdre English
Song: Burning Times by Elaine Silver
Moon phase: Dark moon
Crystal: Black Obsidian

My Vision for October

Tuesday | 1 October 2024 - Waning Crescent

6:00		Today's quick wins
7:00		
8:00		
9:00		
10:00		
11:00		Health and nutrition
12:00		
13:00		
14:00		Today, I am grateful for...
15:00		
16:00		
17:00		Today's self care
18:00		
19:00		
20:00		Chart your cycle
21:00		
22:00		
23:00		Positive affirmation
Notes		

Wednesday | 2 October 2024

New Moon Solar Eclipse in Libra — 18.49 GMT

6:00	**Today's quick wins**
7:00	
8:00	
9:00	
10:00	
11:00	**Health and nutrition**
12:00	
13:00	
14:00	**Today, I am grateful for...**
15:00	
16:00	
17:00	**Today's self care**
18:00	
19:00	
20:00	**Chart your cycle**
21:00	
22:00	
23:00	**Positive affirmation**
Notes	

Thursday | 3 October 2024 - Waxing Crescent

6:00		Today's quick wins
7:00		
8:00		
9:00		
10:00		
11:00		Health and nutrition
12:00		
13:00		
14:00		Today, I am grateful for...
15:00		
16:00		
17:00		Today's self care
18:00		
19:00		
20:00		Chart your cycle
21:00		
22:00		
23:00		Positive affirmation

Notes

Friday | 4 October 2024 - Waxing Crescent

6:00		Today's quick wins
7:00		
8:00		
9:00		
10:00		
11:00		Health and nutrition
12:00		
13:00		
14:00		Today, I am grateful for...
15:00		
16:00		
17:00		Today's self care
18:00		
19:00		
20:00		Chart your cycle
21:00		
22:00		
23:00		Positive affirmation
Notes		

Saturday | 5 October 2024 - Waxing Crescent

6:00		Today's quick wins
7:00		
8:00		
9:00		
10:00		
11:00		Health and nutrition
12:00		
13:00		
14:00		Today, I am grateful for...
15:00		
16:00		
17:00		Today's self care
18:00		
19:00		
20:00		Chart your cycle
21:00		
22:00		
23:00		Positive affirmation

Notes

Sunday | 6 October 2024 - Waxing Crescent

6:00	**Today's quick wins**
7:00	
8:00	
9:00	
10:00	
11:00	**Health and nutrition**
12:00	
13:00	
14:00	**Today, I am grateful for...**
15:00	
16:00	
17:00	**Today's self care**
18:00	
19:00	
20:00	**Chart your cycle**
21:00	
22:00	
23:00	**Positive affirmation**
Notes	

Monday | 7 October 2024 - Waxing Crescent

6:00	**Today's quick wins**
7:00	
8:00	
9:00	
10:00	
11:00	**Health and nutrition**
12:00	
13:00	
14:00	**Today, I am grateful for...**
15:00	
16:00	
17:00	**Today's self care**
18:00	
19:00	
20:00	**Chart your cycle**
21:00	
22:00	
23:00	**Positive affirmation**
Notes	

Tuesday | 8 October 2024 - Waxing Crescent

6:00	**Today's quick wins**
7:00	
8:00	
9:00	
10:00	
11:00	**Health and nutrition**
12:00	
13:00	
14:00	**Today, I am grateful for...**
15:00	
16:00	
17:00	**Today's self care**
18:00	
19:00	
20:00	**Chart your cycle**
21:00	
22:00	
23:00	**Positive affirmation**
Notes	

Wednesday | 9 October 2024 - Waxing Crescent

6:00	Today's quick wins	
7:00		
8:00		
9:00		
10:00		
11:00	Health and nutrition	
12:00		
13:00		
14:00	Today, I am grateful for...	
15:00		
16:00		
17:00	Today's self care	
18:00		
19:00		
20:00	Chart your cycle	
21:00		
22:00		
23:00	Positive affirmation	

Notes

Thursday | 10 October 2024 - First Quarter

6:00		Today's quick wins
7:00		
8:00		
9:00		
10:00		
11:00		Health and nutrition
12:00		
13:00		
14:00		Today, I am grateful for...
15:00		
16:00		
17:00		Today's self care
18:00		
19:00		
20:00		Chart your cycle
21:00		
22:00		
23:00		Positive affirmation
Notes		

Friday | 11 October 2024 - Waxing Gibbous

6:00		**Today's quick wins**
7:00		
8:00		
9:00		
10:00		
11:00		**Health and nutrition**
12:00		
13:00		
14:00		**Today, I am grateful for...**
15:00		
16:00		
17:00		**Today's self care**
18:00		
19:00		
20:00		**Chart your cycle**
21:00		
22:00		
23:00		**Positive affirmation**
Notes		

Saturday | 12 October 2024 - Waxing Gibbous

6:00	**Today's quick wins**
7:00	
8:00	
9:00	
10:00	
11:00	**Health and nutrition**
12:00	
13:00	
14:00	**Today, I am grateful for...**
15:00	
16:00	
17:00	**Today's self care**
18:00	
19:00	
20:00	**Chart your cycle**
21:00	
22:00	
23:00	**Positive affirmation**
Notes	

Sunday | 13 October 2024 - Waxing Gibbous

6:00		Today's quick wins
7:00		
8:00		
9:00		
10:00		
11:00		Health and nutrition
12:00		
13:00		
14:00		Today, I am grateful for...
15:00		
16:00		
17:00		Today's self care
18:00		
19:00		
20:00		Chart your cycle
21:00		
22:00		
23:00		Positive affirmation
Notes		

Monday | 14 October 2024 - Waxing Gibbous

6:00	**Today's quick wins**
7:00	
8:00	
9:00	
10:00	
11:00	**Health and nutrition**
12:00	
13:00	
14:00	**Today, I am grateful for...**
15:00	
16:00	
17:00	**Today's self care**
18:00	
19:00	
20:00	**Chart your cycle**
21:00	
22:00	
23:00	**Positive affirmation**

Notes

Tuesday | 15 October 2024 - Waxing Gibbous

6:00		Today's quick wins	
7:00			
8:00			
9:00			
10:00			
11:00		Health and nutrition	
12:00			
13:00			
14:00		Today, I am grateful for...	
15:00			
16:00			
17:00		Today's self care	
18:00			
19:00			
20:00		Chart your cycle	
21:00			
22:00			
23:00		Positive affirmation	

Notes

Wednesday | 16 October 2024 - Waxing Gibbous

6:00		**Today's quick wins**	
7:00			
8:00			
9:00			
10:00			
11:00		**Health and nutrition**	
12:00			
13:00			
14:00		**Today, I am grateful for…**	
15:00			
16:00			
17:00		**Today's self care**	
18:00			
19:00			
20:00		**Chart your cycle**	
21:00			
22:00			
23:00		**Positive affirmation**	
Notes			

Thursday | 17 October 2024 - Full Moon in Aries 11.26 GMT

6:00	Today's quick wins	
7:00		
8:00		
9:00		
10:00		
11:00	Health and nutrition	
12:00		
13:00		
14:00	Today, I am grateful for...	
15:00		
16:00		
17:00	Today's self care	
18:00		
19:00		
20:00	Chart your cycle	
21:00		
22:00		
23:00	Positive affirmation	
Notes		

Friday | 18 October 2024 - Waning Gibbous

6:00	**Today's quick wins**
7:00	
8:00	
9:00	
10:00	
11:00	**Health and nutrition**
12:00	
13:00	
14:00	**Today, I am grateful for...**
15:00	
16:00	
17:00	**Today's self care**
18:00	
19:00	
20:00	**Chart your cycle**
21:00	
22:00	
23:00	**Positive affirmation**
Notes	

Saturday | 19 October 2024 - Waning Gibbous

6:00		**Today's quick wins**	
7:00			
8:00			
9:00			
10:00			
11:00		**Health and nutrition**	
12:00			
13:00			
14:00		**Today, I am grateful for...**	
15:00			
16:00			
17:00		**Today's self care**	
18:00			
19:00			
20:00		**Chart your cycle**	
21:00			
22:00			
23:00		**Positive affirmation**	

Notes

Sunday | 20 October 2024 - Waning Gibbous

6:00	**Today's quick wins**
7:00	
8:00	
9:00	
10:00	
11:00	**Health and nutrition**
12:00	
13:00	
14:00	**Today, I am grateful for...**
15:00	
16:00	
17:00	**Today's self care**
18:00	
19:00	
20:00	**Chart your cycle**
21:00	
22:00	
23:00	**Positive affirmation**
Notes	

Monday | 21 October 2024 - Waning Gibbous

6:00		**Today's quick wins**
7:00		
8:00		
9:00		
10:00		
11:00		**Health and nutrition**
12:00		
13:00		
14:00		**Today, I am grateful for...**
15:00		
16:00		
17:00		**Today's self care**
18:00		
19:00		
20:00		**Chart your cycle**
21:00		
22:00		
23:00		**Positive affirmation**
Notes		

Tuesday | 22 October 2024 - Waning Gibbous

6:00	**Today's quick wins**
7:00	
8:00	
9:00	
10:00	
11:00	**Health and nutrition**
12:00	
13:00	
14:00	**Today, I am grateful for...**
15:00	
16:00	
17:00	**Today's self care**
18:00	
19:00	
20:00	**Chart your cycle**
21:00	
22:00	
23:00	**Positive affirmation**

Notes

Wednesday | 23 October 2024 - Waning Gibbous

6:00	**Today's quick wins**
7:00	
8:00	
9:00	
10:00	
11:00	**Health and nutrition**
12:00	
13:00	
14:00	**Today, I am grateful for...**
15:00	
16:00	
17:00	**Today's self care**
18:00	
19:00	
20:00	**Chart your cycle**
21:00	
22:00	
23:00	**Positive affirmation**

Notes

Thursday | 24 October 2024 - Last Quarter

6:00	**Today's quick wins**
7:00	
8:00	
9:00	
10:00	
11:00	**Health and nutrition**
12:00	
13:00	
14:00	**Today, I am grateful for...**
15:00	
16:00	
17:00	**Today's self care**
18:00	
19:00	
20:00	**Chart your cycle**
21:00	
22:00	
23:00	**Positive affirmation**

Notes

Friday | 25 October - Waning Crescent

6:00	**Today's quick wins**
7:00	
8:00	
9:00	
10:00	
11:00	**Health and nutrition**
12:00	
13:00	
14:00	**Today, I am grateful for...**
15:00	
16:00	
17:00	**Today's self care**
18:00	
19:00	
20:00	**Chart your cycle**
21:00	
22:00	
23:00	**Positive affirmation**
Notes	

Saturday | 26 October 2024 - Waning Crescent

6:00	**Today's quick wins**
7:00	
8:00	
9:00	
10:00	
11:00	**Health and nutrition**
12:00	
13:00	
14:00	**Today, I am grateful for...**
15:00	
16:00	
17:00	**Today's self care**
18:00	
19:00	
20:00	**Chart your cycle**
21:00	
22:00	
23:00	**Positive affirmation**
Notes	

Sunday | 27 October 2024 - Waning Crescent

6:00		Today's quick wins
7:00		
8:00		
9:00		
10:00		
11:00		Health and nutrition
12:00		
13:00		
14:00		Today, I am grateful for...
15:00		
16:00		
17:00		Today's self care
18:00		
19:00		
20:00		Chart your cycle
21:00		
22:00		
23:00		Positive affirmation

Notes

Monday | 28 October 2024 - Waning Crescent

6:00	**Today's quick wins**
7:00	
8:00	
9:00	
10:00	
11:00	**Health and nutrition**
12:00	
13:00	
14:00	**Today, I am grateful for...**
15:00	
16:00	
17:00	**Today's self care**
18:00	
19:00	
20:00	**Chart your cycle**
21:00	
22:00	
23:00	**Positive affirmation**
Notes	

Tuesday | 29 October 2024 - Waning Crescent

6:00		Today's quick wins
7:00		
8:00		
9:00		
10:00		
11:00		Health and nutrition
12:00		
13:00		
14:00		Today, I am grateful for…
15:00		
16:00		
17:00		Today's self care
18:00		
19:00		
20:00		Chart your cycle
21:00		
22:00		
23:00		Positive affirmation

Notes

Wednesday | 30 October 2024 - Waning Crescent

6:00	**Today's quick wins**
7:00	
8:00	
9:00	
10:00	
11:00	**Health and nutrition**
12:00	
13:00	
14:00	**Today, I am grateful for...**
15:00	
16:00	
17:00	**Today's self care**
18:00	
19:00	
20:00	**Chart your cycle**
21:00	
22:00	
23:00	**Positive affirmation**
Notes	

Thursday | 31 October 2024 - Waning Crescent

Time		Section	
6:00		**Today's quick wins**	
7:00			
8:00			
9:00			
10:00			
11:00		**Health and nutrition**	
12:00			
13:00			
14:00		**Today, I am grateful for...**	
15:00			
16:00			
17:00		**Today's self care**	
18:00			
19:00			
20:00		**Chart your cycle**	
21:00			
22:00			
23:00		**Positive affirmation**	

Notes

October achievements

Be proud of yourself and all that you have achieved this month. Write down your wins, big and small. If you have not achieved everything that you set out to do, that's okay! We learn and grow through our mistakes and experiences. You can use this space to make notes about anything that you have learned.

November 2024

Notes	Monday	Tuesday	Wednesday
	4	5	6
	11	12	13
	18	19	20
	25	26	27

Thursday	Friday	Saturday	Sunday
31	1 ●	2	3
7	8	9 ☽	10
14	15 ○	16	17
21	22 ☾	23	24
28	29	30	1

ARIADNE

Goddess of the moon, stars, labyrinths and mazes.

She represents the spiral of life.

Ariadne used her red thread to help Thesus find his way out of a labyrinth in ancient mythology.
Red thread is also a metaphor used when referring to the energy that binds females to their ancestors. She reminds us of the threads that bind us throughout our human history/herstory, through space and time.

Ariadne can be called upon when we feel lost and the way out is unclear.

Book: Ariadne by Jennifer Saint
Song: The Labyrinth Song by Asaf Avidan
Moon phase: New moon
Crystal: Serpentine

My November Vision

'Doing what you love is the cornerstone of having abundance in your life'
— Dr Wayne Dyer

Friday | 1 November 2024 - New Moon in Scorpio 12.46 GMT

6:00		**Today's quick wins**	
7:00			
8:00			
9:00			
10:00			
11:00		**Health and nutrition**	
12:00			
13:00			
14:00		**Today, I am grateful for...**	
15:00			
16:00			
17:00		**Today's self care**	
18:00			
19:00			
20:00		**Chart your cycle**	
21:00			
22:00			
23:00		**Positive affirmation**	
Notes			

Saturday | 2 November 2024 - Waxing Crescent

6:00		Today's quick wins
7:00		
8:00		
9:00		
10:00		
11:00		Health and nutrition
12:00		
13:00		
14:00		Today, I am grateful for...
15:00		
16:00		
17:00		Today's self care
18:00		
19:00		
20:00		Chart your cycle
21:00		
22:00		
23:00		Positive affirmation

Notes

Sunday | 3 November 2024 - Waxing Crescent

6:00		Today's quick wins
7:00		
8:00		
9:00		
10:00		
11:00		Health and nutrition
12:00		
13:00		
14:00		Today, I am grateful for...
15:00		
16:00		
17:00		Today's self care
18:00		
19:00		
20:00		Chart your cycle
21:00		
22:00		
23:00		Positive affirmation
Notes		

Monday | 4 November 2024 - Waxing Crescent

6:00	Today's quick wins	
7:00		
8:00		
9:00		
10:00		
11:00	Health and nutrition	
12:00		
13:00		
14:00	Today, I am grateful for...	
15:00		
16:00		
17:00	Today's self care	
18:00		
19:00		
20:00	Chart your cycle	
21:00		
22:00		
23:00	Positive affirmation	

Notes

Tuesday | 5 November 2024 - Waxing Crescent

6:00		Today's quick wins
7:00		
8:00		
9:00		
10:00		
11:00		Health and nutrition
12:00		
13:00		
14:00		Today, I am grateful for...
15:00		
16:00		
17:00		Today's self care
18:00		
19:00		
20:00		Chart your cycle
21:00		
22:00		
23:00		Positive affirmation

Notes

Wednesday | 6 November 2024 - Waxing Crescent

6:00	**Today's quick wins**
7:00	
8:00	
9:00	
10:00	
11:00	**Health and nutrition**
12:00	
13:00	
14:00	**Today, I am grateful for...**
15:00	
16:00	
17:00	**Today's self care**
18:00	
19:00	
20:00	**Chart your cycle**
21:00	
22:00	
23:00	**Positive affirmation**
Notes	

Thursday | 7 November 2024 - Waxing Crescent

6:00		**Today's quick wins**	
7:00			
8:00			
9:00			
10:00			
11:00		**Health and nutrition**	
12:00			
13:00			
14:00		**Today, I am grateful for...**	
15:00			
16:00			
17:00		**Today's self care**	
18:00			
19:00			
20:00		**Chart your cycle**	
21:00			
22:00			
23:00		**Positive affirmation**	

Notes

Friday | 8 November - Waxing Crescent

6:00	**Today's quick wins**	
7:00		
8:00		
9:00		
10:00		
11:00	**Health and nutrition**	
12:00		
13:00		
14:00	**Today, I am grateful for...**	
15:00		
16:00		
17:00	**Today's self care**	
18:00		
19:00		
20:00	**Chart your cycle**	
21:00		
22:00		
23:00	**Positive affirmation**	

Notes

Saturday | 9 November 2024 - First Quarter

6:00	**Today's quick wins**
7:00	
8:00	
9:00	
10:00	
11:00	**Health and nutrition**
12:00	
13:00	
14:00	**Today, I am grateful for...**
15:00	
16:00	
17:00	**Today's self care**
18:00	
19:00	
20:00	**Chart your cycle**
21:00	
22:00	
23:00	**Positive affirmation**

Notes

Sunday | 10 November 2024 - Waxing Gibbous

6:00		Today's quick wins
7:00		
8:00		
9:00		
10:00		
11:00		Health and nutrition
12:00		
13:00		
14:00		Today, I am grateful for...
15:00		
16:00		
17:00		Today's self care
18:00		
19:00		
20:00		Chart your cycle
21:00		
22:00		
23:00		Positive affirmation

Notes

Monday | 11 November 2024 - Waxing Gibbous

6:00		**Today's quick wins**	
7:00			
8:00			
9:00			
10:00			
11:00		**Health and nutrition**	
12:00			
13:00			
14:00		**Today, I am grateful for...**	
15:00			
16:00			
17:00		**Today's self care**	
18:00			
19:00			
20:00		**Chart your cycle**	
21:00			
22:00			
23:00		**Positive affirmation**	

Notes

Tuesday | 12 November 2024 - Waxing Gibbous

6:00		**Today's quick wins**
7:00		
8:00		
9:00		
10:00		
11:00		**Health and nutrition**
12:00		
13:00		
14:00		**Today, I am grateful for...**
15:00		
16:00		
17:00		**Today's self care**
18:00		
19:00		
20:00		**Chart your cycle**
21:00		
22:00		
23:00		**Positive affirmation**
Notes		

Wednesday | 13 November 2024 - Waxing Gibbous

6:00		**Today's quick wins**	
7:00			
8:00			
9:00			
10:00			
11:00		**Health and nutrition**	
12:00			
13:00			
14:00		**Today, I am grateful for...**	
15:00			
16:00			
17:00		**Today's self care**	
18:00			
19:00			
20:00		**Chart your cycle**	
21:00			
22:00			
23:00		**Positive affirmation**	

Notes

Thursday | 14 November 2024 - Waxing Gibbous

6:00	**Today's quick wins**
7:00	
8:00	
9:00	
10:00	
11:00	**Health and nutrition**
12:00	
13:00	
14:00	**Today, I am grateful for...**
15:00	
16:00	
17:00	**Today's self care**
18:00	
19:00	
20:00	**Chart your cycle**
21:00	
22:00	
23:00	**Positive affirmation**
Notes	

Friday | 15 November 2024 - Full Moon in Taurus 21.28 GMT

6:00	**Today's quick wins**
7:00	
8:00	
9:00	
10:00	
11:00	**Health and nutrition**
12:00	
13:00	
14:00	**Today, I am grateful for...**
15:00	
16:00	
17:00	**Today's self care**
18:00	
19:00	
20:00	**Chart your cycle**
21:00	
22:00	
23:00	**Positive affirmation**
Notes	

Saturday | 16 November 2024 - Waning Gibbous

6:00		Today's quick wins
7:00		
8:00		
9:00		
10:00		
11:00		Health and nutrition
12:00		
13:00		
14:00		Today, I am grateful for...
15:00		
16:00		
17:00		Today's self care
18:00		
19:00		
20:00		Chart your cycle
21:00		
22:00		
23:00		Positive affirmation
Notes		

Sunday | 17 November 2024 - Waning Gibbous

6:00	**Today's quick wins**
7:00	
8:00	
9:00	
10:00	
11:00	**Health and nutrition**
12:00	
13:00	
14:00	**Today, I am grateful for...**
15:00	
16:00	
17:00	**Today's self care**
18:00	
19:00	
20:00	**Chart your cycle**
21:00	
22:00	
23:00	**Positive affirmation**

Notes

Monday | 18 November 2024 - Waning Gibbous

6:00	**Today's quick wins**
7:00	
8:00	
9:00	
10:00	
11:00	**Health and nutrition**
12:00	
13:00	
14:00	**Today, I am grateful for...**
15:00	
16:00	
17:00	**Today's self care**
18:00	
19:00	
20:00	**Chart your cycle**
21:00	
22:00	
23:00	**Positive affirmation**

Notes

Tuesday | 19 November 2024 - Waning Gibbous

6:00	**Today's quick wins**
7:00	
8:00	
9:00	
10:00	
11:00	**Health and nutrition**
12:00	
13:00	
14:00	**Today, I am grateful for...**
15:00	
16:00	
17:00	**Today's self care**
18:00	
19:00	
20:00	**Chart your cycle**
21:00	
22:00	
23:00	**Positive affirmation**

Notes

Wednesday | 20 November 2024 - Waning Gibbous

6:00		**Today's quick wins**	
7:00			
8:00			
9:00			
10:00			
11:00		**Health and nutrition**	
12:00			
13:00			
14:00		**Today, I am grateful for...**	
15:00			
16:00			
17:00		**Today's self care**	
18:00			
19:00			
20:00		**Chart your cycle**	
21:00			
22:00			
23:00		**Positive affirmation**	

Notes

Thursday | 21 November 2024 - Waning Gibbous

6:00	**Today's quick wins**
7:00	
8:00	
9:00	
10:00	
11:00	**Health and nutrition**
12:00	
13:00	
14:00	**Today, I am grateful for...**
15:00	
16:00	
17:00	**Today's self care**
18:00	
19:00	
20:00	**Chart your cycle**
21:00	
22:00	
23:00	**Positive affirmation**

Notes

Friday | 22 November 2024 - Last Quarter

6:00		Today's quick wins	
7:00			
8:00			
9:00			
10:00			
11:00		Health and nutrition	
12:00			
13:00			
14:00		Today, I am grateful for...	
15:00			
16:00			
17:00		Today's self care	
18:00			
19:00			
20:00		Chart your cycle	
21:00			
22:00			
23:00		Positive affirmation	

Notes

Saturday | 23 November - Last Quarter

6:00		Today's quick wins
7:00		
8:00		
9:00		
10:00		
11:00		Health and nutrition
12:00		
13:00		
14:00		Today, I am grateful for...
15:00		
16:00		
17:00		Today's self care
18:00		
19:00		
20:00		Chart your cycle
21:00		
22:00		
23:00		Positive affirmation

Notes

Sunday | 24 November 2024 - Waning Crescent

6:00	**Today's quick wins**
7:00	
8:00	
9:00	
10:00	
11:00	**Health and nutrition**
12:00	
13:00	
14:00	**Today, I am grateful for...**
15:00	
16:00	
17:00	**Today's self care**
18:00	
19:00	
20:00	**Chart your cycle**
21:00	
22:00	
23:00	**Positive affirmation**

Notes

Monday | 25 November 2024 - Waning Crescent

6:00		**Today's quick wins**
7:00		
8:00		
9:00		
10:00		
11:00		**Health and nutrition**
12:00		
13:00		
14:00		**Today, I am grateful for...**
15:00		
16:00		
17:00		**Today's self care**
18:00		
19:00		
20:00		**Chart your cycle**
21:00		
22:00		
23:00		**Positive affirmation**
Notes		

Tuesday | 26 November 2024 - Waning Crescent

6:00		Today's quick wins
7:00		
8:00		
9:00		
10:00		
11:00		Health and nutrition
12:00		
13:00		
14:00		Today, I am grateful for...
15:00		
16:00		
17:00		Today's self care
18:00		
19:00		
20:00		Chart your cycle
21:00		
22:00		
23:00		Positive affirmation
Notes		

Wednesday | 27 November 2024 - Waning Crescent

6:00	**Today's quick wins**
7:00	
8:00	
9:00	
10:00	
11:00	**Health and nutrition**
12:00	
13:00	
14:00	**Today, I am grateful for...**
15:00	
16:00	
17:00	**Today's self care**
18:00	
19:00	
20:00	**Chart your cycle**
21:00	
22:00	
23:00	**Positive affirmation**
Notes	

Thursday | 28 November 2024 - Waning Crescent

6:00		Today's quick wins
7:00		
8:00		
9:00		
10:00		
11:00		Health and nutrition
12:00		
13:00		
14:00		Today, I am grateful for...
15:00		
16:00		
17:00		Today's self care
18:00		
19:00		
20:00		Chart your cycle
21:00		
22:00		
23:00		Positive affirmation

Notes

Friday | 29 November 2024 - Waning Crescent

6:00	Today's quick wins
7:00	
8:00	
9:00	
10:00	
11:00	Health and nutrition
12:00	
13:00	
14:00	Today, I am grateful for...
15:00	
16:00	
17:00	Today's self care
18:00	
19:00	
20:00	Chart your cycle
21:00	
22:00	
23:00	Positive affirmation
Notes	

Saturday | 30 November 2024 - Waning Crescent

6:00	**Today's quick wins**
7:00	
8:00	
9:00	
10:00	
11:00	**Health and nutrition**
12:00	
13:00	
14:00	**Today, I am grateful for...**
15:00	
16:00	
17:00	**Today's self care**
18:00	
19:00	
20:00	**Chart your cycle**
21:00	
22:00	
23:00	**Positive affirmation**

Notes

November achievements

Be proud of yourself and all that you have achieved this month. Write down your wins, big and small. If you have not achieved everything that you set out to do, that's okay! We learn and grow through our mistakes and experiences. You can use this space to make notes about anything that you have learned.

December 2024

Notes	Sunday	Monday	Tuesday
	1 ●	2	3
	8 ☽	9	10
	15 ○	16	17
	22 ☽	23	24
	29	30 ●	31

Wednesday	Thursday	Friday	Saturday
4	5	6	7
11	12	13	14
18	19	20	21 *Winter Solstice*
25	26	27	28
1	2	3	4

December
Mother Mary

MARY

Mary is honoured by Christians in the Bible and by Muslims in the Quran where she is known as Maryam.

She has inspired artists for centuries, and people travel all over the world to visit her holy shrines.
She couragously travelled many miles whilst heavily pregnant. She gave birth to a son who was gifted frankincense, myrrh and gold. Mary went to great lengths to protect him, even fleeing to Egypt where they would be safe.
Her story plays out today, from the plight of refugees who flee for safety with their young children, to the growing human rights movement around childbirth. We should be free to birth however and wherever we like, free from threats, violence and co-ersion. Mary's free birth in a barn has inspired many of us.

Book: Childbirth as a rite of passage by Dr Rachel Reed
Song: Let it be by The Beatles
Moon phase: Full moon
Crystal: Malachite

My Vision for December

Sunday | 1 December 2024 - New Moon in Sagittarius 06.21 GMT

6:00	**Today's quick wins**
7:00	
8:00	
9:00	
10:00	
11:00	**Health and nutrition**
12:00	
13:00	
14:00	**Today, I am grateful for...**
15:00	
16:00	
17:00	**Today's self care**
18:00	
19:00	
20:00	**Chart your cycle**
21:00	
22:00	
23:00	**Positive affirmation**
Notes	

Monday | 2 December 2024 - Waxing Crescent

6:00	**Today's quick wins**
7:00	
8:00	
9:00	
10:00	
11:00	**Health and nutrition**
12:00	
13:00	
14:00	**Today, I am grateful for...**
15:00	
16:00	
17:00	**Today's self care**
18:00	
19:00	
20:00	**Chart your cycle**
21:00	
22:00	
23:00	**Positive affirmation**
Notes	

Tuesday | 3 December 2024 - Waxing Crescent

6:00	**Today's quick wins**
7:00	
8:00	
9:00	
10:00	
11:00	**Health and nutrition**
12:00	
13:00	
14:00	**Today, I am grateful for...**
15:00	
16:00	
17:00	**Today's self care**
18:00	
19:00	
20:00	**Chart your cycle**
21:00	
22:00	
23:00	**Positive affirmation**
Notes	

Wednesday | 4 December 2024 - Waxing Crescent

6:00	**Today's quick wins**
7:00	
8:00	
9:00	
10:00	
11:00	**Health and nutrition**
12:00	
13:00	
14:00	**Today, I am grateful for...**
15:00	
16:00	
17:00	**Today's self care**
18:00	
19:00	
20:00	**Chart your cycle**
21:00	
22:00	
23:00	**Positive affirmation**
Notes	

Thursday | 5 December 2024 - Waxing Crescent

6:00	**Today's quick wins**
7:00	
8:00	
9:00	
10:00	
11:00	**Health and nutrition**
12:00	
13:00	
14:00	**Today, I am grateful for...**
15:00	
16:00	
17:00	**Today's self care**
18:00	
19:00	
20:00	**Chart your cycle**
21:00	
22:00	
23:00	**Positive affirmation**
Notes	

Friday | 6 December 2024 - Waxing Crescent

6:00		Today's quick wins	
7:00			
8:00			
9:00			
10:00			
11:00		Health and nutrition	
12:00			
13:00			
14:00		Today, I am grateful for…	
15:00			
16:00			
17:00		Today's self care	
18:00			
19:00			
20:00		Chart your cycle	
21:00			
22:00			
23:00		Positive affirmation	
Notes			

Saturday | 7 December 2024 - Waxing Crescent

6:00	**Today's quick wins**
7:00	
8:00	
9:00	
10:00	
11:00	**Health and nutrition**
12:00	
13:00	
14:00	**Today, I am grateful for...**
15:00	
16:00	
17:00	**Today's self care**
18:00	
19:00	
20:00	**Chart your cycle**
21:00	
22:00	
23:00	**Positive affirmation**

Notes

Sunday | 8 December - First Quarter

6:00	**Today's quick wins**
7:00	
8:00	
9:00	
10:00	
11:00	**Health and nutrition**
12:00	
13:00	
14:00	**Today, I am grateful for...**
15:00	
16:00	
17:00	**Today's self care**
18:00	
19:00	
20:00	**Chart your cycle**
21:00	
22:00	
23:00	**Positive affirmation**
Notes	

Monday | 9 December 2024 - Waxing Gibbous

6:00		**Today's quick wins**	
7:00			
8:00			
9:00			
10:00			
11:00		**Health and nutrition**	
12:00			
13:00			
14:00		**Today, I am grateful for...**	
15:00			
16:00			
17:00		**Today's self care**	
18:00			
19:00			
20:00		**Chart your cycle**	
21:00			
22:00			
23:00		**Positive affirmation**	

Notes

Tuesday | 10 December 2024 - Waxing Gibbous

6:00	**Today's quick wins**
7:00	
8:00	
9:00	
10:00	
11:00	**Health and nutrition**
12:00	
13:00	
14:00	**Today, I am grateful for...**
15:00	
16:00	
17:00	**Today's self care**
18:00	
19:00	
20:00	**Chart your cycle**
21:00	
22:00	
23:00	**Positive affirmation**
Notes	

Wednesday | 11 December 2024 - Waxing Gibbous

6:00		**Today's quick wins**	
7:00			
8:00			
9:00			
10:00			
11:00		**Health and nutrition**	
12:00			
13:00			
14:00		**Today, I am grateful for...**	
15:00			
16:00			
17:00		**Today's self care**	
18:00			
19:00			
20:00		**Chart your cycle**	
21:00			
22:00			
23:00		**Positive affirmation**	
Notes			

Thursday | 12 December 2024 - Waxing Gibbous

6:00	**Today's quick wins**
7:00	
8:00	
9:00	
10:00	
11:00	**Health and nutrition**
12:00	
13:00	
14:00	**Today, I am grateful for...**
15:00	
16:00	
17:00	**Today's self care**
18:00	
19:00	
20:00	**Chart your cycle**
21:00	
22:00	
23:00	**Positive affirmation**
Notes	

Friday | 13 December 2024 - Waxing Gibbous

6:00		Today's quick wins
7:00		
8:00		
9:00		
10:00		
11:00		Health and nutrition
12:00		
13:00		
14:00		Today, I am grateful for...
15:00		
16:00		
17:00		Today's self care
18:00		
19:00		
20:00		Chart your cycle
21:00		
22:00		
23:00		Positive affirmation
Notes		

Saturday | 14 December 2024 - Waxing Gibbous

6:00	**Today's quick wins**
7:00	
8:00	
9:00	
10:00	
11:00	**Health and nutrition**
12:00	
13:00	
14:00	**Today, I am grateful for...**
15:00	
16:00	
17:00	**Today's self care**
18:00	
19:00	
20:00	**Chart your cycle**
21:00	
22:00	
23:00	**Positive affirmation**

Notes

Sunday | 15 December 2024 - Full Moon in Gemini 09.01 GMT

6:00	Today's quick wins	
7:00		
8:00		
9:00		
10:00		
11:00	Health and nutrition	
12:00		
13:00		
14:00	Today, I am grateful for...	
15:00		
16:00		
17:00	Today's self care	
18:00		
19:00		
20:00	Chart your cycle	
21:00		
22:00		
23:00	Positive affirmation	
Notes		

Monday | 16 December 2024 - Waning Gibbous

6:00	**Today's quick wins**
7:00	
8:00	
9:00	
10:00	
11:00	**Health and nutrition**
12:00	
13:00	
14:00	**Today, I am grateful for...**
15:00	
16:00	
17:00	**Today's self care**
18:00	
19:00	
20:00	**Chart your cycle**
21:00	
22:00	
23:00	**Positive affirmation**
Notes	

Tuesday | 17 December 2024 - Waning Gibbous

6:00		**Today's quick wins**
7:00		
8:00		
9:00		
10:00		
11:00		**Health and nutrition**
12:00		
13:00		
14:00		**Today, I am grateful for...**
15:00		
16:00		
17:00		**Today's self care**
18:00		
19:00		
20:00		**Chart your cycle**
21:00		
22:00		
23:00		**Positive affirmation**

Notes

Wednesday | 18 December 2024 - Waning Gibbous

6:00		**Today's quick wins**	
7:00			
8:00			
9:00			
10:00			
11:00		**Health and nutrition**	
12:00			
13:00			
14:00		**Today, I am grateful for...**	
15:00			
16:00			
17:00		**Today's self care**	
18:00			
19:00			
20:00		**Chart your cycle**	
21:00			
22:00			
23:00		**Positive affirmation**	
Notes			

Thursday | 19 December 2024 - Waning Gibbous

6:00		Today's quick wins
7:00		
8:00		
9:00		
10:00		
11:00		Health and nutrition
12:00		
13:00		
14:00		Today, I am grateful for…
15:00		
16:00		
17:00		Today's self care
18:00		
19:00		
20:00		Chart your cycle
21:00		
22:00		
23:00		Positive affirmation
Notes		

Friday | 20 December 2024 - Waning Gibbous

6:00	**Today's quick wins**
7:00	
8:00	
9:00	
10:00	
11:00	**Health and nutrition**
12:00	
13:00	
14:00	**Today, I am grateful for...**
15:00	
16:00	
17:00	**Today's self care**
18:00	
19:00	
20:00	**Chart your cycle**
21:00	
22:00	
23:00	**Positive affirmation**
Notes	

Saturday | 21 December 2024 - Waning Gibbous

6:00		**Today's quick wins**	
7:00			
8:00			
9:00			
10:00			
11:00		**Health and nutrition**	
12:00			
13:00			
14:00		**Today, I am grateful for...**	
15:00			
16:00			
17:00		**Today's self care**	
18:00			
19:00			
20:00		**Chart your cycle**	
21:00			
22:00			
23:00		**Positive affirmation**	
Notes			

Sunday | 22 December 2024 - Last Quarter

6:00	**Today's quick wins**
7:00	
8:00	
9:00	
10:00	
11:00	**Health and nutrition**
12:00	
13:00	
14:00	**Today, I am grateful for...**
15:00	
16:00	
17:00	**Today's self care**
18:00	
19:00	
20:00	**Chart your cycle**
21:00	
22:00	
23:00	**Positive affirmation**
Notes	

Monday 23 December - Last Quarter

6:00		Today's quick wins
7:00		
8:00		
9:00		
10:00		
11:00		Health and nutrition
12:00		
13:00		
14:00		Today, I am grateful for...
15:00		
16:00		
17:00		Today's self care
18:00		
19:00		
20:00		Chart your cycle
21:00		
22:00		
23:00		Positive affirmation
Notes		

Tuesday | 24 December 2024 - Waning Crescent

6:00	**Today's quick wins**
7:00	
8:00	
9:00	
10:00	
11:00	**Health and nutrition**
12:00	
13:00	
14:00	**Today, I am grateful for...**
15:00	
16:00	
17:00	**Today's self care**
18:00	
19:00	
20:00	**Chart your cycle**
21:00	
22:00	
23:00	**Positive affirmation**
Notes	

Wednesday | 25 December 2024 - Waning Crescent

6:00	**Today's quick wins**
7:00	
8:00	
9:00	
10:00	
11:00	**Health and nutrition**
12:00	
13:00	
14:00	**Today, I am grateful for...**
15:00	
16:00	
17:00	**Today's self care**
18:00	
19:00	
20:00	**Chart your cycle**
21:00	
22:00	
23:00	**Positive affirmation**
Notes	

Thursday | 26 December 2024 - Waning Crescent

6:00		Today's quick wins	
7:00			
8:00			
9:00			
10:00			
11:00		Health and nutrition	
12:00			
13:00			
14:00		Today, I am grateful for...	
15:00			
16:00			
17:00		Today's self care	
18:00			
19:00			
20:00		Chart your cycle	
21:00			
22:00			
23:00		Positive affirmation	
Notes			

Friday | 27 December 2024 - Waning Crescent

6:00	**Today's quick wins**
7:00	
8:00	
9:00	
10:00	
11:00	**Health and nutrition**
12:00	
13:00	
14:00	**Today, I am grateful for...**
15:00	
16:00	
17:00	**Today's self care**
18:00	
19:00	
20:00	**Chart your cycle**
21:00	
22:00	
23:00	**Positive affirmation**
Notes	

Saturday | 28 December 2024 - Waning Crescent

6:00	**Today's quick wins**
7:00	
8:00	
9:00	
10:00	
11:00	**Health and nutrition**
12:00	
13:00	
14:00	**Today, I am grateful for...**
15:00	
16:00	
17:00	**Today's self care**
18:00	
19:00	
20:00	**Chart your cycle**
21:00	
22:00	
23:00	**Positive affirmation**

Notes

Sunday | 29 December 2024 - Waning Crescent

6:00	**Today's quick wins**
7:00	
8:00	
9:00	
10:00	
11:00	**Health and nutrition**
12:00	
13:00	
14:00	**Today, I am grateful for...**
15:00	
16:00	
17:00	**Today's self care**
18:00	
19:00	
20:00	**Chart your cycle**
21:00	
22:00	
23:00	**Positive affirmation**
Notes	

Monday | 30 December 2024 - New Moon in Capricorn 22.26 GMT

6:00	**Today's quick wins**
7:00	
8:00	
9:00	
10:00	
11:00	**Health and nutrition**
12:00	
13:00	
14:00	**Today, I am grateful for...**
15:00	
16:00	
17:00	**Today's self care**
18:00	
19:00	
20:00	**Chart your cycle**
21:00	
22:00	
23:00	**Positive affirmation**
Notes	

Tuesday | 31 December 2024 - Waxing Crescent

6:00	**Today's quick wins**
7:00	
8:00	
9:00	
10:00	
11:00	**Health and nutrition**
12:00	
13:00	
14:00	**Today, I am grateful for...**
15:00	
16:00	
17:00	**Today's self care**
18:00	
19:00	
20:00	**Chart your cycle**
21:00	
22:00	
23:00	**Positive affirmation**

Notes

December achievements

Be proud of yourself and all that you have achieved this month. Write down your wins, big and small. If you have not achieved everything that you set out to do, that's okay! We learn and grow through our mistakes and experiences. You can use this space to make notes about anything that you have learned.

What have I achieved and how have I grown in 2024...

My 2024 Reading List

Film & Podcast Notes

Notes

Notes

Notes

Vision for 2025

www.ingramcontent.com/pod-product-compliance
Lightning Source LLC
Chambersburg PA
CBHW071651220426
43209CB00100BB/992